BOOGIE NIGHTS

BOOGIE NIGHTS

Paul Thomas Anderson

faber and faber

First published in 1998
by Faber and Faber Limited
3 Queen Square London WC1N 3AU

Photoset by Parker Typesetting Service, Leicester
Printed in England by Clays Ltd, St Ives plc

A CIP record for this book
is available from the British Library

ISBN 0-571-19539-3

2 4 6 8 10 9 7 5 3 1

CONTENTS

INTRODUCTION

So here is this script which I suppose, technically, was ten years in the making. When I was seventeen – young, impressionable and horny – I wrote a short film called 'The Dirk Diggler Story.' I shot it on video and it was fun and actually pretty good.

What was I doing for the ten years I was trying to write this script? Well, I was accidentally devising what I think is an interesting method. The short film was a fictional documentary, basically a *Spinal Tap* and *Zelig* rip-off. A couple years later, when I was nineteen, I expanded the short into a feature, keeping the structure of a fictional documentary. Well, by that time, the format, so wonderfully done so many times, had, in fact, 'been done so many times.'

I spent a couple years getting over that format and decided to write a straight narrative. So when approaching the first draft, I was basically adapting a documentary. It worked wonderfully for me to have a sort of 'bible' to reference whenever I felt myself getting lost in so many stories and so many ideas.

I want to note a couple of (some obvious) sources of inspiration and would urge anyone who hasn't seen these films to see them as soon as you can. Stop reading this stupid introduction and see these films: *Battle of Algiers* (Pontecorvo), *Nashville* (Altman), *GoodFellas* (Scorsese), *Singin' in the Rain* (Donen), *Shoot the Piano Player*, *Jules and Jim* (Truffaut), *Putney Swope* (Downey, Sr.), *42nd Street* (Bacon), *The Jade Pussycat* (Chinn). These are pictures which not only influenced and inspired me to make films but were really templates (all in odd and various stages), massive life-preservers in the writing of *Boogie Nights*.

The script you have in your hands is the one we went to the set with every day. You will see that some stuff is shot exactly as written and you will notice that some stuff has changed. The changes, by a large percent, are the result of having brilliant actors who have me, the biggest geek fan of their work, laughing at any and all bits of improv that they could muster. If you hire John C. Reilly, Don Cheadle, Phil Hoffman, Mark Wahlberg, Luis

Guzman, Heather Graham, Bob Ridgely, Julianne Moore, Burt Reynolds, Melora Walters, Ricky Jay, Bill Macy, Thomas Jane and Alfred Molina, the best thing to do is sit back and enjoy all that they give.

I've come to realize that my function as a director is to be a good writer. My *obligation* as a director is to deliver the actors a good script, thus making my job as a director describable as 'hanging out' and watching them go. No good actor needs direction beyond 'Let's do another one' and 'Keep it simple.'

I hope one thing that is clear is that this script is not written like a book. In other words, this is a script not a novel. In other words, there is no description of behavior. In other words, there is no flour and sugar. In other words, this is a script written for actors. An actor does not need a full description of their character. They do not need: 'Angela, thirtyish and hot as hell. I mean real hot, hot like the Noxema girl (if you know what I mean). She walks smoothly and with a flair for the exceptional into the room, and then looks longingly at her hands, remembering that her father once told her, "You're a bad girl."' This is how most screenplays are written. This sort of thing must be written by writers who have no interest in meeting or socializing with actors. If you have written this and you can find an actress to play this part, as described, you will have a bad actress. Actors do not need this, they do not want it. Don't give it to them; they will not read it anyway. This is writing for studio executives. Studio executives do not make movies. They pretend that they make movies. This is a script written for the people who *really* make the movie, people who physically put it into existence, and all they need are the facts. Pure and Simple.

There are two sequences in the script that are fairly important to the *script*, but in the end were not very important to the *picture*. They are the Becky/Jerome/Dirk's Car sequence (sc. 138–146) and Dirk's return home to Sheryl Lynn (sc. 182–185). We shot these bits and they were wonderful, but in an effort to focus the storytelling, I cut them. I miss them only when I see them, but I sure don't miss them when I'm watching the film.

The 'Sequences' that you'll see listed through the script were mile markers for the production crew. It's a system that I formed from ripping off a more complicated system that Preston Sturges devised in structuring his shooting scripts. Each Sequence, marked by letters, usually meant that some very specific piece of music was being used and we should all pay attention to that vibe. It translated into costume design stuff (more color, less color), camera moves (fast, slow, with zooms, high or low contrast, etc.) and a general handle on how the film would structure. Sequence D was our favorite because it was a free-for-all. No matching. No rules. No anything. D for debauchery, D for drugs, D for down, D for do anything.

I wrote three drafts of *Boogie Nights*. This is the final shooting script. The 'pink pages' (noted with asterisks next to the scene) or rewrites are stuff that I did either right before shooting as a result of something in rehearsals or as a result of budgetary/scheduling conflicts.

A few people to thank for this script and its publication: John Lesher, Joanne Sellar, Walter Donohue, Mike DeLuca, Lynn Harris, Lloyd Levin, Wendy Weidman, Dylan Tichenor, Paula Chavez.

If you liked the movie, I hope you like the script. If you didn't like the movie, this script isn't going to help much.

P. T. Anderson
12 December, 1997
Los Angeles, California

BOOGIE NIGHTS

1   <u>EXT. HOT TRAXX NIGHTCLUB - NIGHT</u>   1

CAMERA holds on this PACKED disco on Van Nuys Blvd.

TITLE CARD: "San Fernando Valley, 1977"

A CADILLAC SEVILLE pulls up to the valet area and CAMERA (STEADICAM) moves across the street, towards the car, landing in close;

From the Seville steps, JACK HORNER (50s) and AMBER WAVES (early 30s) CAMERA follows them (this is one continuous shot) as they pass the crowd, greet a DOORMAN and enter --

INSIDE THE NIGHTCLUB. Twice as packed inside as outside. Music is full blast. Amber and Jack are greeted by;

MAURICE t.t. RODRIGUEZ (30s) Owner of the nightclub. Puerto Rican. Wearing a suit and fifteen gold chains.

> MAURICE
> Jackie-Jack-Jack and Miss Lovely Amber Waves --

> AMBER
> Hi, Maurice.

> JACK
> You bad ass little spick. How are you, honey?

> MAURICE
> Pissed off you ain't been around --

> JACK
> -- I been on vacation.

> MAURICE
> Don't stay away this long from my
> club ever again, Jackie-Jack-Jack.

> JACK
> I promise.

Maurice takes Amber's hand and gives it a kiss.

> MAURICE
> You are the foxiest bitch in ten counties.

> AMBER
> You're such a charmer.

> MAURICE
> (to Jack)
> I got you all set up at your booth. ·
> I wanna send over some clams on the half shell.

> JACK
> Beautiful.

                    MAURICE
          Just remember, Jack: I'm available
          and ready. Cast me and find out --

                    JACK
          Yeah,yeah,yeah.

Amber and Jack head off towards the booth. CAMERA stays with Maurice,
follows him to the bar area, where he shouts some orders to a WAITER.

                    MAURICE
          Clams on the half shell to Jack
          and Amber -- over there -- go!

The WAITER takes off to the kitchen, Maurice walks onto the dance
floor and greets three people;

REED ROTHCHILD, 20s, tall and skinny, BECKY BARNETT, 20s,
black girl in silk, BUCK SWOPE, 20s, black guy in cowboy gear.

                    MAURICE
          Hello there, kiddies.

                    REED/BUCK/BECKY
          Hi, hey, hi, Maurice.

                    MAURICE
          Having a good time?

                    BECKY
          Excellent.

                    MAURICE
          Great, great, great.

Maurice moves away to greet some more people. CAMERA stays with Reed,
Becky and Buck, does a 360 around them. Reed and Becky Disco Dance.
Buck does some Cowboy-Type Moves.

Moments later, the WAITER carrying clams on the half shell passes
and CAMERA picks up with him, follows him to Jack's booth, where he
presents them;

                    WAITER
          Compliments of Maurice.

                    JACK
          Thank you.

                    AMBER
          Can I get a Marguerita, please?

                    JACK
          Seven-Up, here --

The WAITER exits, CAMERA PANS with him for a moment, leading to a
young girl wearing rollerskates, ROLLERGIRL (aged 18) She always,
<u>always</u> wears rollerskates. CAMERA PANS with her back to Jack's booth.

                    ROLLERGIRL
          Hi.

                    JACK
          Hello, honey.

                    AMBER
                (to Rollergirl)
          Did you call that girl today?

                    ROLLERGIRL
          I forgot.

                    AMBER
          If you don't do it tomorrow, then it's
          the weekend and you'll never be able to
          get in to see her --

                    ROLLERGIRL
          OK.

Rollergirl scratches her crotch as she speaks. Amber notices;

                    AMBER
          What's the matter down there?

                    ROLLERGIRL
          I gotta go pee.

                    AMBER
          Well go, then.

CAMERA stays with Rollergirl, following her across the dance floor.
She passes Buck, Becky and Reed, says hello, dances a moment,
then continues on -- into the clearing off the dance floor, heading
for the bathroom. She passes something, CAMERA moves away towards
this something:

A bus boy cleaning a table, EDDIE ADAMS, aged 17. CAMERA moves into
a CU -- blending to SLOW MOTION (40fps) for a moment.

(Note: In the text Eddie Adams will be referred to as <u>Dirk Diggler</u>.)

ANGLE, JACK'S TABLE.
Jack turns his head, looks across the dance floor and sees this
kid cleaning the table.

ANGLE, DIRK DIGGLER.
he looks up, catches Jack looking back at him, then turns away,
disappears into a back room.

CAMERA DOLLIES in on Jack, who at that moment, is approached by
a figure entering FRAME. Short, buffed out LITTLE BILL (late 40s.)
This is Jack's Assistant Director.

                    LITTLE BILL
          Jack.

                    JACK
          Hey, Little Bill.

                    LITTLE BILL
          Whatsa schedule look like?
          Are we still on day after tomorrow?

                    JACK
          I wanna do it the day after
          the day after tomorrow.

                    LITTLE BILL
          For sure? 'Cause I wanna call
          Rocky, Scotty, Kurt and all those guys --

Jack's attention is with the backroom that Dirk entered.
He stands and heads away.

                    JACK
          Absolutely. But I wanna keep it small.
          I wanna keep a small crew on this one --

                    LITTLE BILL
          -- a relaxed deal.

                    JACK
          Exactly.

                    LITTLE BILL
          Do you have a script yet?

                    JACK
          Tomorrow. Tomorrow is the day --

Jack is off across the dance floor.
                                        CUT TO:

2   INT. BACKROOM/KITCHEN - MOMENTS LATER   2

> JACK
> Hey.   *
>   *

> DIRK
> Hey.   *
>   *

> JACK
> How ya doin'?   *
>   *

> DIRK
> Fine.   *
>   *

> JACK
> How old are you?   *
>   *

> DIRK
> I have a work permit, I got the paper --   *
>   *

> JACK
> No, no, no. Not like that.   *
> How long have you worked here?   *
>   *

> DIRK
> A month.   *
>   *

> JACK
> Maurice give you a job here?   *
>   *

> DIRK
> Yeah.   *
>   *

> JACK
> How much he pay you?   *
>   *

> DIRK
> I'm not supposed to say how much I make.   *
>   *

> JACK
> He's a friend of mine --   *
>   *

> DIRK
> Well you'll have to ask him.   *
>   *

> JACK
> You live around here, Canoga - Reseda?   *
>   *

> DIRK '
> Um...no....do you know where Torrance is?   *
>   *

> JACK
> How do you get here?   *
>   *

                              DIRK   *
          I take the bus.   *

                         JACK   *
          So what do you wanna do?   *

                              DIRK   *
          What?   *

                         JACK   *
          You take the bus from Torrance to work   *
          in Reseda, why don't you work in Torrance?   *

                              DIRK   *
          I don't want to.   *

                         JACK   *
          ...ok...   *

                              DIRK   *
          So....you want five or ten?   *

                         JACK   *
          ...what...?   *

                              DIRK   *
          If you wanna watch me jack off   *
        ' it's ten bucks. If you just wanna   *
          look at it then it's five.   *

                         JACK   *
          Guys come in, ask you to jack off   *
          for them, ask to see it?   *

                              DIRK   *
          Yeah.   *

                         JACK   *
          Have you done it tonight?   *

                              DIRK   *
          Couple times.   *

                         JACK   *
          And you can do it again?   *

                              DIRK   *
          If you want, if you got ten bucks.   *

     BEAT. Jack extends his hand...   *

                         JACK   *
          I'm Jack.   *

                         DIRK   *
          Eddie. Eddie Adams.   *

                         JACK   *
          Eddie Adams from Torrance. I'm Jack   *
          Horner, Filmmaker.   *

                         DIRK   *
          Really?   *

                         JACK   *
          I make adult films. Erotic pictures.   *

BEAT, THEN;   *

                         DIRK   *
          ...I know who you are. I read about you *
          in a magazine. "Inside Amber," "Amanda's *
          Ride." You made those --   *

                         JACK   *
          So you know me, you know I'm not full   *
          of doggy-do-do --   *

                         DIRK   *
          Yeah....   *

                         JACK   *
          So why don't you come back   *
          to my table, have a drink,   *
          meet some people --   *

                         DIRK   *
          I'd love to but...I'm working --   *

                         JACK   *
          You need money, you have to pay the rent -- *

                         DIRK   *
          ...No...I mean, yeah. I need money.   *
          But I don't pay rent. I live at home.   *

                         JACK   *
          Tell me how old you are, Eddie.   *

                         DIRK   *
          ...I'm seventeen.....   *

                         JACK   *
          You're a seventeen year old piece of gold. *

                              DIRK   *
         Yeah, right.   *

                              JACK   *
         Why don't you come back to my table,   *
         have a drink, meet some people --   *

                              DIRK   *
         I can't do that to Maurice.   *

                              JACK   *
         You're a good worker, yeah?   *

                              DIRK   *
         I'm sorry, I do know you, I know   *
         who you are, I'd love to have a drink   *
         with you and I know you're not   *
         full of --   *

                              JACK   *
         -- doggy-doo-doo.   *

                              DIRK   *
         Yeah, yeah. But I just can't   *
         walk out on Maurice. I'm sorry.   *

BEAT, THEN;   *

                              JACK   *
         It seems to me, beneath those jeans,   *
         there's something wonderful just   *
         waiting to get out --   *

Jack leaves.   *

                                              CUT TO:*

PAGE 9 AND PAGE 10 HAVE BEEN OMITTED.   *

3   EXT. HOT TRAXX NIGHTCLUB - NIGHT (LATER)   3

The club is closing, Maurice is locking up and turning the lights
off out front. CAMERA hangs around with Buck, Becky and Reed.
(Director's Note: Reference improv. notes)

Jack and Amber cruise past in his Seville, say so long and head
up Van Nuys Blvd.

They pass Little Bill who walks to his old Station Wagon, rips
· a parking ticket off the windshield and gets behind the wheel.

Dirk Diggler exits the club from a side door and heads off --

                                              CUT TO:

4   OMITTED   4

5   INT. JACK'S HOUSE/LAUREL CANYON - NIGHT - LATER   5

Jack and Amber enter the house. It resembles the Jungle Room
at Graceland. He heads for the kitchen, she makes a drink...

                        JACK
              You want somethin' to eat?
              I'm onnamake some eggs.

                        AMBER
              I'm goin' to sleep.

                        JACK
              Goodnight, honey-tits. Sleep beautiful.

                                              CUT TO:

6   INT. AMBER'S BEDROOM/JACK'S HOUSE - NIGHT - MOMENTS LATER 6

ECU, AMBER. She does a quick line of coke. BEAT. She takes
a valium, lights a cigarette, then picks up the phone;

                        AMBER
              Tom...hi...yeah. I know it's late, but...
                        (beat)
              Yeah. Is Andy there? Is he...?
              I'd like to say hello, I'd like to say
              hello to my son and that's all.
                        (beat)
              Lemme tell you something, Tom.
              Lemme tell you something you don't know;
              I know a lawyer, you understand?
              You might think I don't but I do
              and I'll take you to court....
                        (beat)
              No...please don't, Tom, Tom, Tom --

Dial tone from the phone. She hangs up.

7   INT. LITTLE BILL'S HOUSE - NIGHT   7

   Little Bill enters his house quietly, turns on a small light to help
   guide him down a hallway.

   FROM A BEDROOM DOOR we hear the sounds of MOANING AND GROANING.
   Little Bill walks to the door, hesitates, then opens --

                                                    CUT TO:

8   INT. LITTLE BILL'S BEDROOM - NIGHT - THAT MOMENT   8

   LITTLE BILL'S WIFE and a BIG STUD are doing it on the bed.
   They stop a moment and casually look at him.

                         LITTLE BILL
               What the fuck are you doing?

                         LITTLE BILL'S WIFE
               The fuck does it look like I'm doing?
               I've got a cock in my pussy, you idiot.

                         BIG STUD
               Will you close the door?

                         LITTLE BILL
               Will I close the door? You're fucking
               my wife, asshole.

                         BIG STUD
               Relax, little man.

                         LITTLE BILL'S WIFE
               Just get out, Bill. Fucking sleep on the couch.
                    (to Big Stud)
               Keep going, Big Stud.

   Big Stud continues. Little Bill watches a moment in a haze then
   closes the door.

                                                    CUT TO:

9   INT. DIRK'S PARENTS HOUSE/TORRANCE - NIGHT   9

   Dirk enters quietly, walks a hallway and goes into his room.

                                                    CUT TO:

10   INT. DIRK'S ROOM - NIGHT - THAT MOMENT   10

      Dirk enters his room and begins to removes his clothes. He turns
      the volume low on his stereo. He stands in front of his mirror,
      does a few flexes, some dance moves, some karate moves, etc.
      CAMERA DOES A SLOW 360 PAN AROUND THE ROOM. Posters on the walls
      of Travolta, Pacino, a 1976 Corvette, Bruce Lee, Hawaii, a Penthouse
      centerfold, Luke Skywalker, etc. CAMERA LANDS BACK ON DIRK;

                              DIRK
                  That's right.

                                             FADE OUT, CUT TO:

11   OMITTED   11

12   OMITTED   12

13   INT. DIRK'S HOUSE/KITCHEN - MORNING   13

      Dirk eats breakfast. His MOTHER (mid 40s) stands, washing a dish.
      His FATHER (50s) enters, dressed in suite. He crosses the kitchen

      INSERT, CU.
      Father, stubble on his face, places a kiss on the cheek of Mother.

                              FATHER
                  Good morning.

                              MOTHER
                  ...Jesus. Please, okay? Shave if you're
                  gonna do that, it scratches my face.

      Father takes a seat at the breakfast table, looks to Dirk.

                              FATHER
                  How's that work, you get home late, huh?

                              DIRK
                  Yeah.

                              MOTHER
                  If you wanna work in a nightclub you
                  should...if it's so important...you
                  should find one closer.

                              DIRK
                  ...yeah...

      They eat in silence.

                              DIRK
                  I've gotta get to work.

                              MOTHER
                  ...at a car wash...

                          DIRK
          What?

                          MOTHER
          You work at a car wash, school never
          occured to you?

     Dirk stands up, places his plates in the sink and exits.

    .   CUT TO:

14   OMITTED   14

15   OMITTED   15

16   INT. HIGH SCHOOL CLASSROOM - DAY   16

     A crowded high school geometry classroom. In the back of the class,
     sitting at a desk is Rollergirl. A TEACHER walks about, handing
     out the final exam. Rollergirl looks it over; a lot of questions,
     diagrams and generally confusing material. She looks across the room;

     Two BOYS are looking at her and chuckling to themselves.
     One guy looks to the other and makes a "blow job" gesture.

     She looks away, they continue their gestures and giggling.
     Other students notice and smile.

     CAMERA ARRIVES CU. ON ROLLERGIRL. She stands up, heads for the
     door -- the teacher calls after her -- but she's gone.

                                                CUT TO:

17   INT. SUPER-DUPER STEREO SHOP - DAY   17

     A semi-high end stereo store in the valley. Buck, dressed in his
     usual cowboy-digs, is talking to a CUSTOMER about a stereo unit.
     The manager, a skinny-white guy with a mustache and mustard suit,
     JERRY (30s) is standing nearby.

                          BUCK
          -- so basically you're gettin'
          twice the bass, cause of the TK421
          modification we got in this system here.

                          CUSTOMER
          I don't know - do I need that much bass?

                          BUCK
          If you want a system to handle
          what you want -- yes you do.
          See this system here. This is Hi-Fi.
          "High Fidelity." What that means is
          that it's the highest quality fidelity.

                         CUSTOMER
          It's the price --

                         BUCK
          I have this unit at home.

                         CUSTOMER
          ...really...?

                         BUCK
          Yes. But -- I've got it modified
          with the TK421, which is a bass unit
          that basically kicks in another two,
          maybe three quads when you really
          crank -- lemme put another eight track
          in so you can get a better idea what
          I'm talkin about --

Buck ejects the Eight Track that was playing and puts in his
own of a country western song.

                         BUCK
          Hear that bass? It kicks and turns
          and curls up in your belly, makes you
          wanna freaky-deaky, right? If you get
          this unit as it is -- it won't sound
          like this without the modification --
          and we do that for a small price.

The Customer listens another moment, then;

                         CUSTOMER
          Thank you for your time.

                         BUCK
          No problem.

The Customer exits and Jerry approaches Buck.

                         JERRY
          ...the fuck was that?

                         BUCK
          Wha?

                         JERRY
          Have I told you? Huh? Have I?

                         BUCK
          What? I don't --

                              JERRY
              Alright: A.) You play that country
              western-crap and no one's gonna buy
              a stereo. You throw on some KC and
              the Sunshine Band, a guy looks a particular
              way -- and you've seen the profile sheet --
              you throw on some Led Zepplin. No.
              Instead, you play this twingy-twangy,
              yappy-dappy music. What kinda brother
              are you anyway, listening to that shit?

                              BUCK
              Hey, Jerry, look --

                              JERRY
              No _you_ look. I gave you a job here
              because I thought your film work
              might bring some nice pussy in the
              place -- and it has -- but I can't
              have anymore fuck ups -- you dig?

                              BUCK
              Yeah.

                              JERRY
              Alright. Go unload the new 484's
              from the backroom.

          Buck goes to the backroom.

                                                      CUT TO:

18   INT. SHERYL LYNN'S BEDROOM - DAY - LATER   18

          Dirk is in bed with a young neighborhood girl, SHERYL LYNN PARTRIDGE.
          Her room is decorated in pastels with equestrian things all around.
          Horse models, trophies from riding, blue ribbons, etc.

                              DIRK
                  I have to get back.

                              SHERYL LYNN
                  Once more.

                              DIRK
                  I have to get back to work.

                              SHERYL LYNN
                  Give it to me, Eddie.

                              DIRK
                  Don't make me pounce you, Sheryl Lynn.

                              SHERYL LYNN
                  Ohhhh-baby, baby, baby.

                    DIRK
          I'll do it --

                    SHERYL LYNN
          Promise?

                    DIRK
          That's it.

Dirk jumps up and starts bouncing up and down on the bed,
naked and flapping. She stares at his crotch, shakes her head;

                    DIRK (OC)
          What?

                    SHERYL LYNN
          You're so beautiful.

                    DIRK (OC)
          Yeah...

                    SHERYL LYNN
          Do you know how good you are at
          doing this, Eddie? Having sex...fucking me...
          making love to me?

Dirk looks down. BEAT.

                    DIRK
          Everyone has one thing, y'think? I mean:
          Everyone is given one special thing....right?

                    SHERYL LYNN
          That's right.

                    DIRK
          Everyone is blessed with One Special Thing.

Dirk kneels down to her;

                    DIRK
          I want you to know: I plan on being a star.
          A big, bright shinning star. That's what
          I want and it's what I'm gonna get.

                    SHERYL LYNN
          I know.

                    DIRK
          And once I get it: I'm never gonna stop
          and I'll never, ever make a mistake.

They Kiss.

                                        CUT TO:

19   INT. HOT TRAXX NIGHTCLUB - NIGHT   19

      Nightclub is in full swing on a Friday Night. CAMERA hangs with
      Dirk for a while as he buses tables.

      ANGLE, JACK'S BOOTH.
      Rollergirl comes over to speak with Jack. He whispers something
      in her ear. She nods, "I understand," and rolls away --

                                                        CUT TO:

20   INT. HOT TRAXX/HALLWAY - NIGHT - THAT MOMENT   20

      CAMERA follows on the heels of the rollerskates as they move down
      the hallway and into --

      THE KITCHEN
      Dirk is washing dishes. He looks up and spots Rollergirl. She lifts
      a skate up just a little...she rolls closer to Dirk and pulls him into

      A CLOSET SPACE
      She goes down on him, unzips his pants and pulls out his cock.
      She hesitates. DOLLY IN CLOSE ON HER FACE. She smiles up at Dirk.

                                                        CUT TO:

21   OMITTED   21 *

22   EXT. HOT TRAXX NIGHTCLUB - NIGHT - LATER   22

      Closing hour. Dirk exits a side door and starts walking.
      Jack, Amber and Rollergirl in the Seville pull along side him;

                          JACK
              Hey. Eddie.

                          DIRK
              Hello. Jack?

                          JACK
              Yeah. You wanna ride?

                          DIRK
              I'm goin' pretty far.

                          ROLLERGIRL
              You remember me? Couple hours ago?

                    DIRK
          Yeah...I remember you.

                    AMBER
          Come with us, sweetie.

                    DIRK
          Okay.

. Dirk gets in the backseat of the car with Rollergirl.

                                          CUT TO:

23   INT. CANDY'S COFFEE SHOP - NIGHT - LATER   23

     In a booth, after the meal. Dirk and Rollergirl on one side,
     Jack and Amber on the other.

                    JACK
          This thing here, I mean, you understand
          one thing and that's this: It costs.
          I mean, this stuff costs good 'ol American
          Green. You got film, you got lights,
          you got sound, lab fees, developing, synching,
          editing -- next you thing you know you're
          spending thirty/forty thousand a picture.

                    DIRK
          That's a lot of money.

                    JACK
          Hell yes it's a lot of money, but lemme
          tell you something else: You make a good
          film and there's practically no end to the
          amount of money you can make, Eddie.

                    AMBER
          Have you seen Jack's house?

     CAMERA HOLDS ON AMBER. She watches Dirk.

                    DIRK (OC)
          No.

                    JACK (OC)
          He'll see it.

                    ROLLERGIRL (OC)
          He'll see it.

                    JACK (OC)
          Eddie: You got ten, fifteen people around
          and that's just to make sure the lighting is
          right...shit, this is not an operation for
          the weak, and lemme tell you something else:
          When all is said and done, you gotta have the
          juice, you understand? I mean...you can work
          on your arms, your legs, workout morning, day,
          noon, night, the whole deal, but when it comes
          right down to it...what we need is Mr. Torpedo
          Area, y'understand? Mr. Fun Zone? Okay, let's
          say you got that: right? And You Do Got, Yeah?

He looks to Rollergirl. She smiles. CAMERA OFF AMBER NOW.

                    JACK
          I can go out -- tonight -- the reputation
          I got: I can find myself 15/20 guys,
          cocks the size of Willie Mayes Baseball Bat:
          Do I want that: No. Do I need that: No.
          I need actors.

                    AMBER
          Uhhh-ohhh....here we go --

                    JACK
          -- Alright, yeah, I need the big dick,
          and the big tits -- that GETS them in
          the theater. What keeps them in their
          seats even after they've come? Huh?
          The beauty and the acting.
          If you're able to give it up and show the world:
          No, not just your cock: Fuck that.
          What I'm talking about is showing your
          insides, from your heart...you understand?
          Hey, Sure: GET THEM IN THE THEATER.
          That's one thing. I don't want 'em showing up,
          sitting down, jacking off and splitting on
          the story. I don't want to make that film.
          I wanna make the thing that keeps 'em around
          even after they've come....what happens when
          you come? You're done, you wanna split.
          My idea, my goal: Suck 'em in with
          the story...they'll squirt their load and
          sit in it...Just To See How The Story Ends.
          Sometimes we make these films, we wanna
          make people laugh a little, then get into
          it and fuck heavy: That's good and that's fine.
          But I got a dream of a making a film
          that's true...true and right and dramatic.

                    DIRK
          ...Right...right...I understand.

                    AMBER
          Don't listen to hard to all this,
          honey...it's just nice in theory.

                         JACK
          It's a dream to be able to find
          a cock and an actor.

                       ROLLERGIRL
          Dream,dream,dream,dream,dream.

                         DIRK
          If you don't have dreams you have nightmares.

     HOLD. Amber, Jack and Rollergirl look at Dirk.

                                                    CUT TO:

24   INT. JACK'S HOUSE/LIVING ROOM - NIGHT   24

     CAMERA DOES A 180 AROUND THE MAIN PART OF THE HOUSE, LANDS THE
     ANGLE WITH DIRK. He's sitting on a couch, hands folded across
     his lap. OC we hear Jack, Rollergirl and Amber moving about and
     talking.

                       JACK (OC)
          Did you want a Fresca, Eddie?   *
                                                              *
                         DIRK   *
          No thanks.   *

                         JACK   *
          You're sure....?   *

                     ROLLERGIRL (OC)
          ...you're out of limes, Jack.

                       JACK (OC)   *
          Check in the studio fridge....   *
                                                              *

*

                        AMBER (OC)
          I'm going to bed.

                        JACK (OC)
          Good night, honey.

                        AMBER (OC)
          Good night, Jackie. Don't stay up too late.
          Good night, Eddie. I'm glad you came by.

She leans into FRAME and gives Dirk a good-night kiss.

                        AMBER
          You're great.

                        DIRK
          Thank you.

CAMERA PANS WITH AMBER AND LEADS TO AN ANGLE WITH JACK. HOLD.

                        JACK
          She's the best, Eddie. A mother.
          A real and wonderful mother to all
          those who need love.

                        DIRK (OC)
          She's really nice.

                        JACK
          So what do you think...I think
          we ought to be in business together.

                        DIRK (OC)   *
          ...yeah...?   *
                                                      *
                        JACK
          What do you think of Rollergirl?

                        DIRK (OC)
          She's...she's really great...

                        JACK
          Would you like to get it on with her?

                        DIRK (OC)
          Have sex?

                    JACK
          Yeah.

                    DIRK (OC)
          Yeah. I'd love to. I mean, yes.
          She's...she's really foxy.

                    JACK
          Bet your ass she is --

Rollergirl enters back into the house. CAMERA SWING PANS OVER:

                    ROLLERGIRL
          You're officially out of limes, Jack.

                    JACK
          I'll get you some more tomorrow.
          Come over here a minute. Sit next
          to Eddie on the couch there.

                    ROLLERGIRL
          Here We Go! Are We Gonna Fuck?

                    JACK
          Yes you are.

                    ROLLERGIRL
          Oh, wait,wait,wait, then.

She rolls over to the Hi-Fi System and picks a record.
She sets the needle on the turntable and rolls over to
the couch -- in one swift motion ripping her clothes off.

                    ROLLERGIRL
          You ready?

                    DIRK
          Are you?

                    ROLLERGIRL
          Ohhh-yeah.

They kiss. They lean back on the couch. Dirk stops a moment.

                    DIRK
          Are you gonna take your skates off?

                    ROLLERGIRL
          I don't take my skates off.

                    DIRK
          Okay.

                    ROLLERGIRL
          Don't fucking come in me.

                              JACK
                    Don't come in her, Eddie. I want you
                    to pull it out and jack off, make sure
                    you aim it towards her face.

                            ' ROLLERGIRL
                    Fuck you, Jack.

                              JACK
                    Towards her tits, then.

          CAMERA HOLDS ON JACK. OC sounds of Dirk and Rollergirl making
          out on the couch. SLOW ZOOM INTO CU. ON JACK.

                                                      CUT TO:

   25   INT. DIRK'S HOUSE - EARLY MORNING - LATER   25

          Dirk enters quietly, walks down the hallway, passing the kitchen.
          His MOTHER is there, looking at him. HOLD, THEN:
                              DIRK
                    Hi.

                              MOTHER
                    Where were you?

                              DIRK
                    Nowhere.

                              MOTHER
                    Shut-up. Shut-up. Where were you?

          Dirk walks down the hall towards his room.

                              MOTHER
                    You see that little slut girl you see?
                    Sheryl? Sheryl Lynn?

                              DIRK
                    Don't say that.

                              MOTHER
                    Does it make you feel like a stud to
                    see trash like that? Huh? What is she?
                    Your _girl_-friend?

                              DIRK
                    She's not my girlfriend.

                              MOTHER
                    She's a little whore and a little
                    piece of trash...I know you're not .
                    the only one that she sees.

                              DIRK
                    What...what're you...you don't know.

                              MOTHER
                    I've heard things about her. That girl.
                    Don't think I don't know what goes on
                    when I'm not here...I wash your sheets, kid.
                    I know she's been here. Or are you doing
                    some other thing in there? With your
                    music and your posters on the wall?

                                                        CUT TO:

26   INT. BEDROOM - MORNING - THAT MOMENT   26

      Dirk's FATHER is sitting on the edge of his bed, listening
      to the fight outside.

                              MOTHER (OC)
                    Why don't you go to your little whore,
                    Sheryl Lynn. Your little GIRL-FRIEND.

                              DIRK (OC)
                    Maybe I will.

                              MOTHER (OC)
                    Oh yeah? Yeah, what are you gonna do?

                              DIRK (OC)
                    I dunno, I'll do something.

                                                        CUT TO:

27   INT. HALLWAY - MORNING - THAT MOMENT   27

                              MOTHER
                    You can't do anything. You're a loser.
                    You'll always be a loser -- you couldn't
                    even finish high school because you were
                    too stupid -- so what are you gonna do?

                              DIRK
                    I'll do something...I'll do it.
                    I'll go somewhere and do something,
                    maybe I'll run away were you can
                    never find me.

                              MOTHER
                    Go ahead. Go ahead and fuck
                    that little GIRL.

      Dirk heads for his room, Mother follows.

                                                        CUT TO:

INT. DIRK'S BEDROOM - MORNING - THAT MOMENT

Dirk heads for a drawer and starts to grab some clothes.

                    MOTHER
          What do you think you're doing?

                    DIRK
          I'm getting my stuff --

                    MOTHER
          -- you think that's your stuff?
          That's not your stuff...you didn't pay
          for that -- it's not yours because
          you didn't pay for it, stupid.

Dirk stops. His Mother looks to the posters on his wall.

                    MOTHER
          None of this stuff is yours. This:

She starts to rip his posters from the wall. Dirk stands.
CAMERA begins a SLOW DOLLY INTO CU.

                    MOTHER (OC)
          If you're gonna leave, you leave with what
          you've got: Nothing. Y'see...you treat me
          like this and this is what you get.
          That's fair. Huh? You wanna live that way?
          Fuck that little whore. I've taken care of
          you all your miserable fucking life....

CAMERA ARRIVES CU. ON DIRK. He's starting to cry.

                    MOTHER (OC)
          ...you pay for it...you owe me for all the
          shit I've done for you in your life....you
          little fucker...you understand? Think you're
          gonna be this? Huh? These god damn posters --
          you're not gonna be this -- you're gonna
          be shit...because you're stupid.

                    DIRK
          I'm not stupid.

                    MOTHER
          Yes you are.

                    DIRK
          Why are you so mean to me? You're my mother...

                    MOTHER
          Not by choice.

                    DIRK
          Don't. Don't be mean to me.

                    MOTHER
          You little fucker, I'm not being mean
          to you, you're just too stupid to see.

                     DIRK
          You don't know what I can do. You don't
          know what I can do or what I'm gonna do
          or what I'm gonna be. You don't know.
          I'm good. I have good things that you
          don't know and I'm gonna be something --
          you -- You Don't Know And You'll See.

                    MOTHER
          You can't do anything.
          You'll never do anything --

                     DIRK
          Don't be mean to me.

                    MOTHER
          YOU LITTLE FUCKER, I'M NOT BEING MEAN TO YOU.

     Dirk CHARGES at his Mother and SLAMS her against the wall.

                     DIRK
          AND YOU DON'T BE MEAN, AND YOU DON T
          TALK TO ME....NO.

                                        CUT TO:

29   EXT. DIRK'S HOUSE/TORRANCE - MORNING   29

     Dirk CHARGES out of the house and runs off down the street.
     Mother appears in the doorway, watches him leave, slams the door --

                                        CUT TO:

30   OMITTED   30 *

31   OMITTED   31 *

32   OMITTED   32

33   INT. JACK'S HOUSE - DAY   33

    Jack, Amber, Rollergirl, Reed, Buck and Becky. They're setting   *
    up for a pool party. Cases of beer, soda and chips all around.

    Dirk comes walking up towards the front door...Jack opens up,   *
    CAMERA PUSHES IN...Jack opens his arms;   *
    *

                         JACK
               Eddie Adams from Torrance! You made it,
               you made it, my darling, come on in here
               I want you to meet someone --

    CAMERA follows with Jack and Dirk as they move to the pool area and
    find Reed, who's setting up the bar

                         JACK
               Reed, honey I want you to meet
               a New Kid On The Block, Eddie Adams.

                         DIRK
               Hi...I'm Eddie....

                         REED
               Hi, Eddie. I'm Reed. You live on this block?

                         DIRK
               No, no.

                         REED
               Oh, I thought Jack said you did.
               You wanna drink?

                         DIRK
               Sure.

                         JACK
               Eddie I want you to hang out for
               a while, I don't want you leaving
               this party...understand me?

                         DIRK
               Sure.

    Jack leaves. Reed looks to Dirk.

                         REED
               Marguerita?

                         DIRK
               Great.

    BEAT. Reed fixes the drink.

                    REED
          Can I ask you something?

                    DIRK
          Uh-huh.

                    REED
          Do you work out?

                    DIRK
          Yeah.

                    REED
          You look like it. Whadda you squat?

                    DIRK
          Two.

                    REED
          Super, super.

                    DIRK
          You?

                    REED
          Three.

                    DIRK
          Wow.

                    REED
          No b.s. Where do you work out?

                    DIRK
          Torrance. In Torrance, where I live.

                    REED
          Cool. Cool. You ever go to Vince's out
          here -- no you couldn't, I would've seen you.

                    DIRK
          I've always wanted to work out at Vince's.

                    REED
          Here we go....taste that.

Dirk sips the Marguerita.

                    DIRK
          Rock and Roll.

                    REED
          Thanks. What do you bench?

                    DIRK
          You tell me first.

                              REED
                    You first.

                              DIRK
                    Same time.

                              REED
                    Cool.

                              DIRK
                    Ready?

                              REED
                    Ready.

                              DIRK/REED
                    One...Two...Three....

SILENCE.

                              DIRK
                    You didn't say it...

                              REED
                    ...neither did you.

ANGLE, POLAROID CAMERA.
it sits on a table top. It's suddenly snapped up by Rollergirl.
CAMERA follows her and the Polaroid out to the pool area where
she snaps photos of Reed and Dirk. (Flash to Developed Polaroids.)

                                                  CUT TO:

34   EXT. JACK'S DRIVEWAY - AFTERNOON - LATER   34 *

      The driveway is PACKED with cars now and the party is in full swing.
      A Big Black Cadillac comes down the driveway. A LIMO DRIVER gets out,
      moves to the back and opens the door. From the car steps:

      THE COLONEL JAMES (mid-60s) Heavy-set in a tan suit. Wrap around
      sunglasses. The Porno Film Distributor. His LADY FRIEND (aged 16)
      steps from the car and smiles;

                              COLONEL
                    You look great, honey.

                              LADY FRIEND
                    Is there gonna be coke at this party, Colonel?

                              COLONEL
                    Yes.

      Jack is right there to greet the Colonel.

                              JACK
                    Colonel, hello and welcome!

                         COLONEL
          Hello, Jack. This is my Lady Friend.

                         JACK
          Hello, darling.

                         LADY FRIEND
          Do you have coke at this party?

                         JACK
          Well I'm sure we can find you some.

                         COLONEL
          Find her some coke, Jack.

                         JACK
          We will, we will. Thanks for coming by.

They exit. CAMERA follows the Limo Driver into the pool area --

                                             CUT TO:

35   EXT. POOL AREA/JACK'S HOUSE - THAT MOMENT   35

CAMERA follows the Limo Driver for a while, then moves away,
to find; Maurice and Amber. They're sitting down, speaking.

                         MAURICE
          ..y'see, Miss Amber, I'm just a poor fellow
          from Puerto Rico. I have the club, yes,
          that's one thing...but soon...the club goes...
          I die...and what do I have? I've got nothing.

                         AMBER
          Uh-huh.

                         MAURICE
          I want something to send back home.
          Something to send back to my brothers and say:
          Look At Me. Look At The Women I've Been With.

                         AMBER
          So what...do you want me to talk to him?

                         MAURICE
          Yes...I mean...y'know...what do you
          think I'm askin' here?

                         AMBER
          ...you wanna be in a movie?

                         MAURICE
          Please. Tell him I won't be bad. Please.

                         AMBER
          I'll see what I can do.

CAMERA moves away, through the party, to find Buck and Becky.

                    BECKY
          ..because it's old...it's old deal.

                    BUCK
          Lemme tell you something:

                    BECKY
          He was obviously pissed about the music.

                    BUCK
          What's wrong with it, y'know?

                    BECKY
          Look, Buck: The cowboy look ended
          about six years ago --

                    BUCK
          -- it's comin' back.

                    BECKY
          No it's not. It's over, it's dead.

                    BUCK
          You don't know what you're talkin' about.

                    BECKY
          I'm just saying and it seems like your
          boss at the stereo store is saying the
          same thing --

                    BUCK
          -- what, what?

                    BECKY
          Get a new look.

                    BUCK
          Yeah...yeah...yeah...you get a new look.

                    BECKY
          The look I've got is just fine.

                    BUCK
          What's your look?

                    BECKY
          Chocolate Love, Baby.

                    BUCK
          Yeah, right.

OC we hear the new song start to play.

                    BECKY
          OH SHIT! TURN IT UP! I LOVE THIS SONG!

Becky leaves. CAMERA moves away to find:

The Colonel's Lady Friend approaches a Young Stud, who's wearing
bikini-speedos and holding court over a table of coke.

>   LADY FRIEND
>   Excuse me...?

>   YOUNG STUD
>   Yes?

>   LADY FRIEND
>   May I please join in?

>   YOUNG STUD
>   Most certainly.

                                        CUT TO:

36   EXT. JACK'S HOUSE/DRIVEWAY - DAY - MOMENTS LATER   36

Little Bill and his Wife get out of his Station Wagon and enter
the party from the driveway. She's dressed up. He's dressed down.

>   LITTLE BILL
>   Just don't embarrass me, alright?

>   LITTLE BILL'S WIFE
>   Fuck you, Bill.

>   LITTLE BILL
>   I work with these people, alright?
>   These are my co-workers, so just --

>   LITTLE BILL'S WIFE
>   Bite it.

>   LITTLE BILL
>   Don't make me do something?

>   LITTLE BILL'S WIFE
>   Ohhhh....I'm so scared.

She moves away. Rollergirl passes and takes a SNAPSHOT.

CU. THE POLAROID - DEVELOPED
Little Bill in a sort of angry-confused-surprised face.

>   ROLLERGIRL
>   What's wrong Little Bill?

>   LITTLE BILL
>   Nothing. How are you Rollergirl?

>   ROLLERGIRL
>   I'm fine.

                         LITTLE BILL
              Is Jack around?

                         ROLLERGIRL
              He's in the house.

Little Bill leaves. CAMERA follows Rollergirl around as she
mingles and snaps more Polaroids.

                                                      CUT TO:

37   INT. JACK'S OFFICE - DAY - THAT MOMENT   37

      Jack and the Colonel are sitting, drinks in their hand.
      The Colonel smokes a cigar.

                         JACK
              The idea is this: Amber is a director
              of porno films and she's down on her luck.
              She hasn't had a hit in a year.
              She's desperate. Her landlord is
              threatening to kick her out, so she's
              desperate for a big dick hit, right?

                         COLONEL
              Yes. Good dilemma.

                         JACK
              Yes. So she calls up all the agencies
              in town and says: "Send over your best
              actors, I'm casting a porno picture."
              Well the story goes and develops with
              Amber auditioning various men and
              women...the whole thing wraps up with
              the Landlord, I'd like to get Jeremy if
              he's still in town to play the part --
              he comes in -- the landlord says:
              You better pay rent or you're through.
              Well: Amber does one helluva suck job,
              ass fuck-come in the face-sort of thing
              and fade out - the end.

                         COLONEL
              That's great.

                         JACK
              There's a kid, a young man, I met him
              last night: His name is Eddie Adams.
              He's here, he's at the party. He's something
              special and I want to cast him.

                         COLONEL
              What films has he done?

                         JACK
              This would be his first.

Little Bill pokes his head into the office, sees the conversation and quickly apologizes and exits. The Colonel looks to Jack;

                    COLONEL
          Casting is up to you, Jack. You wanna do it?
          Then do it. If it has big tits, tight pussy
          and focus: I'm happy. You tell the stories
          you wanna tell, make yourself happy.

                                                  CUT TO:

38   EXT. JACK'S HOUSE/POOL AREA - DAY - THAT MOMENT   38

Reed and Dirk are swimming. Dirk gets up on the diving board.

                    REED
          Do a cannonball.

                    DIRK
          No, no. Watch this Jacknife.

Dirk runs and jumps --

                    DIRK
          JACKNIFE.

He lands in the pool and swims to the surface.

                    DIRK
          How did it look?

                    REED
          Great. Check this out.
               (gets on the board)
          This is gonna be a full-flip.

Reed runs, jumps, goes for the flip but land FLAT ON HIS BACK.

                                                  CUT TO:

39   INT. POOL/UNDERWATER - THAT MOMENT   39

Reed lands. CAMERA moves in on his face. He's in SERIOUS PAIN.
He floats down for a moment....

                                                  CUT TO:

40   EXT. POOL AREA - THAT MOMENT   40

Everyone at the party is looking...holding their breath
and waiting...Reed comes to the surface.
                    REED
          Ouch.

The party people turns back to their conversations...

                         DIRK
             You gotta try and bring your legs
             all the way around...
                         REED
             Yeah.

                                                    CUT TO:

41   INT. JACK'S HOUSE/THE PARTY - DAY - THAT MOMENT   41

     CAMERA follows behind Little Bill. He's walking around,
     looking for his Wife. He greets a few people here and there.

     He runs into a big guy, ROCKY (late 30s.) He's a CREW member.

                         LITTLE BILL
             How you doin' Rocky?

                         ROCKY
             Good, good, what's wrong?

                         LITTLE BILL
             Nothin'. Nothin' at all.

                         ROCKY
             Do you have the schedule for the shoot, or...?

                         LITTLE BILL
             Yeah. You're on.

                         ROCKY
             Is it here?

                         LITTLE BILL
             Yeah, it's gonna be here, but it's a simple one....

     CAMERA picks up with the Lady Friend and the Young Stud with the
     coke...ZOOM after them down a long hallway towards a BEDROOM door.
     They close the door in the CAMERA'S FACE.

                                                    CUT TO:

42   INT. JACK'S KITCHEN - DAY - THAT MOMENT   42

     Maurice and Buck are talking;

                         MAURICE
             Hey, hey, hey, my point is this:

                         BUCK
             What?

                         MAURICE
             You know what I say?

                    BUCK
          What-What?

                    MAURICE
          Wear What You Dig.

The PHONE RINGS. Maurice picks up the phone.

                    MAURICE
          Hello?
                    (beat)
          I'm sorry...I can't hear you
          that well...say again....? Maggie?
                    (to Buck)
          Is there a Maggie here?

                    BUCK
          I don't know a Maggie.

                    MAURICE
                    (into phone)
          I think you might have the wrong number.....
          Your mother? I'm sorry...wait...just...wait...

Maurice sets the phone down, looks to Buck.

                    MAURICE
          Watch that a minute....

CAMERA follows him as he walks out to the pool area --

                    MAURICE
                    (calls out)
          Is there a Maggie here?

No one at the pool area responds so he walks back inside
to the phone. Buck is still watching it closely.

                    MAURICE
                    (into phone)
          I'm sorry...there's no Maggie here.
          Okay...okay...no problem...Bye.

                    BUCK
          What was it?

                    MAURICE
          Some kid lookin' for his mother.

                                        CUT TO:

INT. BATHROOM/JACK'S HOUSE - THAT MOMENT

Amber is sitting in the bathroom, on the toilet. She reaches
to the window, sets aside the curtains and looks.

AMBER'S POV: Looking out to the pool area. Dirk dives off the board
and does a perfect FLIP in SLOW MOTION.

                                                  CUT TO:

44   EXT. JACK'S HOUSE/DRIVEWAY - MOMENTS LATER   44

CAMERA follows Little Bill. He spots six people in a semi-circle
around something. He walks over -- inside the semi-circle, on the
pavement, Little Bill's Wife is getting fucked by some BIG DUDE.

                    LITTLE BILL
          ..the fuck are you doing?

She looks up at him, smiles.

                    WATCHER #1
          What does it look like they're doing?

                    LITTLE BILL
          That's my wife.

                    LITTLE BILL'S WIFE
          Shut-up, Bill.

                    WATCHER #2
          Yeah, shut-up, Bill.

The other WATCHER'S join in telling Little Bill to "Shut-up."
He walks away and CAMERA follows him until he's approached
by a big man, KURT LONGJOHN (late 40s) He's the cameraman.

                    KURT LONGJOHN
          Little Bill.

                    LITTLE BILL
          Hey. Kurt. What's up?

                    KURT LONGJOHN
          What's wrong with you?

                    LITTLE BILL
          ah...my fuckin' wife, man, she's
          over there...she's got some idiot's
          dick in her, people standing around
          watching -- it's a fuckin' embarrassment.

                    KURT LONGJOHN
          Yeah. Yeah. I know. ·Anyway, listen:

                    LITTLE BILL
          -- yeah.

                    KURT LONGJOHN
For the shoot -- I wanna talk about the look.
I wanted to see about getting this new zoom lens....

                    LITTLE BILL
Right.

                    KURT LONGJOHN
I wondered if we'd be able to look into
getting some more lights, too, y'know --

                    LITTLE BILL
Jack wants a minimal-thing --

                    KURT LONGJOHN
Right, well, very often, minimal means
a lot more photographically than I think,
well...then I think most people understand...

                    LITTLE BILL
I understand.

                    KURT LONGJOHN
No, no. Hey. I know you understand,
I was talking about some other people.

                    LITTLE BILL
Well, I think what Jack is talking
about is minimal, not really "natural,"
but minimal...

                    KURT LONGJOHN
OK....fine...I was just saying....

                    LITTLE BILL
I understand --

                    KURT LONGJOHN
-- 'cause I'm just trying to give each
picture it's own look --

                    LITTLE BILL
Can we talk about this later?

                    KURT LONGJOHN
Oh, yeah...you have to go somewhere...or...?

                    LITTLE BILL
Well, no, yeah...I mean....

                    KURT LONGJOHN
'Cause I was hoping to, y'know, for the
shoot tomorrow, we could send Rocky down
and he could pick it up --

                    LITTLE BILL
          Kurt.

                    KURT LONGJOHN
          No. Hey. Gotcha. You've gotta go somewhere
          so -- hey -- what the fuck? It's only the
          photography of the movie we're talkin' about --

Little Bill looks at him. HOLD.

                    LITTLE BILL
          Are you givin' me shit, Kurt?

                    KURT LONGJOHN
          NO, NO, HEY. No way, Little Bill.

                    LITTLE BILL
          My fucking wife has a cock in her ass over
          in the driveway, alright? I'm sorry if my
          thoughts aren't with the photography of the
          film we're shooting tomorrow, Kurt. OK?

                    KURT LONGJOHN
          OK. No big deal. Sorry.

                    LITTLE BILL
          Alright?

                    KURT LONGJOHN
          Gotcha.

Little Bill leaves. Kurt stands alone a moment. He walks over
to the driveway and watches Little Bill's Wife get fucked.

                                                  CUT TO:

45   INT. JACK'S HOUSE/HALLWAY - DAY - LATER   45

     CAMERA follows HAND-HELD behind Jack, the Colonel and his Limo
     Driver as they walk quickly down a hallway that leads to a bedroom.

                                                  CUT TO:

46   INT. BEDROOM - THAT MOMENT   46

     Jack, the Colonel and Limo Driver BURST into the room --

     REVERSE ANGLE: On the floor of the room, the Colonel's LADY FRIEND
     is lying naked. She's passed out and she has blood pouring from her
     nose. The YOUNG STUD is naked, holding her in his arms. He looks
     up at the men who just entered.

                    YOUNG STUD
          I think she's sick.

                    COLONEL
          What the fuck is this?

                    YOUNG STUD
          I didn't do anything.

                    JACK
          Is she breathing?

                    YOUNG STUD
          I don't know. I think she did too much coke?

                    COLONEL
          Duh. Do you think so, smarty?

                    LIMO DRIVER
          She's definitely overdosing.

                    COLONEL
          Oh....what the fuck....

The four men look at the girl. The Colonel turns to his Limo Driver.

                    COLONEL
          Alright: Johnny. You're gonna take care
          of this for me. You listening here?

                    LIMO DRIVER
          Yeah.

                    COLONEL
          I want you pick her up, get her in
          the car, take her down to St. Joe's.

                    LIMO DRIVER
          Okay.

                    COLONEL
          Listen, though: You drop her off in
          the front, I don't want this...y'understand?
          I don't need this, here.

                    LIMO DRIVER
          Gotcha.

                    COLONEL
          Make sure no one see's the limo.

                    LIMO DRIVER
          Got it.

                    COLONEL
          Young Stud, I want you to help my driver
          Johnny here get her in the car.

The Young Stud starts to cry hysterically.

                          COLONEL
                          (to Jack)
              What the fuck is this?
                          (to Young Stud)
              Hey...hey...pal...get a grip, man.

                          YOUNG STUD
              I'm sorry...it's just...it's just....

                          COLONEL
              What?

                          YOUNG STUD
              I...I...I....

                          COLONEL
              Spit it out.

                          YOUNG STUD
              This is twice in two days a chick
              has O.D.'d on me.

                          COLONEL
              Well maybe that means you oughta think about
              getting some new shit, what do you think?

                          YOUNG STUD
              Yes, sir.

                          COLONEL
              Jesus Christ. Now be a man, deal with the
              situation and get her in the car.

      The Lady Friend starts to go into CONVULSIONS.

                          COLONEL
              Y'see that, all this fuckin' conversation --

                          YOUNG STUD
              Please don't die!

                          LIMO DRIVER
              C'mon, pal.

      The Limo Driver and Young Stud carry her naked, convulsing body
      to the Black Limo out front. CAMERA holds with Jack and the Colonel.

                          JACK
              Close call.

                          COLONEL
              Yes.

      They exit.

                                                      CUT TO:

CAMERA is with Reed and Dirk. They're sitting in two pool chairs,
drinking their drinks and talking. A nervous young kid in red
swimming trunks, SCOTTY J. (mid-20s) comes over and interjects --

                         SCOTTY J.
            Hey Reed.

                         REED
            Hey -- Scotty, how are you?

                         SCOTTY J.
            Y'know, y'know.
                   (re: Dirk)
            Who's this?

                         REED
            Eddie -- meet Scotty J. He's a friend,
            he works on some of the films.

                         DIRK
            Nice to meet you.

                         SCOTTY J.
            You too. Are you gonna be working?

                         DIRK
            Maybe.

                         REED
            Probably.

                         SCOTTY J.
            That's great. That's great. Where did
            you meet, Jack? 'Cause I work on the films,
            y'know, sometimes, that's why I'm wondering
            if you, you know --

                         JACK (OC)
            EDDIE! EDDIE! Come over a minute.

Dirk spots Jack calling him and stands, looks to Scotty J.

                         DIRK
            Excuse me.

                         SCOTTY J.
            Yeah, okay.

                         DIRK
            Nice to meet you.

CAMERA DOLLIES IN A LITTLE ON SCOTTY J.

                         REED (OC)
            You wanna take a seat, Scotty?

                    SCOTTY J.
        Um....I dunno...is it alright?

                    REED (OC)
        Yeah.

                    SCOTTY J.
        Thank you. It gets a little hard
        mingling around...y'know...talking to
        people and stuff...it's sort of --
        That kid Eddie is really good looking, huh?

ANGLE, JACK, THE COLONEL AND DIRK.
Dirk approaches and the Colonel smiles. They shake hands.

                    JACK
        This young man is interested
        in the business.

                    COLONEL
        Well, you're in good hands if you
        get involved with Jack, here.

                    DIRK
        Oh, yeah?

                    COLONEL
        I can't give you much advice that Jack
        probably doesn't know, but I can advise,
        maybe you think about your name....?

                    DIRK
        My name...yeah...?

                    COLONEL
        Think about something that makes you happy,
        something that also gives some pizzaz...y'know?

                    DIRK
        Right.

                    JACK
        The Colonel pays for all our films, Eddie.
        He's an important part of the process.

                    DIRK
        Well, great. Great.

                    COLONEL
        I look forward to seeing you in action.
        Jack says you've got a great big coçk.

                    DIRK
        ..um...yeah, I dunno, I guess?

                         COLONEL
               Can I see it?

                         DIRK
               Really?

                         COLONEL
               Please.

Dirk unzips his pants. CAMERA on the Colonel. He looks down, then up;

                         COLONEL
               Thank you, Eddie.

                         DIRK
               No problem.

Dirk exits. The Colonel turns to Jack;

                         COLONEL
               Jesus Christ. Jesus Lord in Heaven.

CAMERA picks up with Dirk, who runs for the pool and DIVES IN.....

                                                      CUT TO:

48   INT. POOL - THAT MOMENT   48

      CAMERA MOVES IN AS DIRK LANDS IN THE WATER, FLOATS TO THE BOTTOM,
      THEN PUSHES OFF, TOWARDS THE SURFACE. TIME LAPSE TO NIGHT.

                                                      CUT TO:

49   EXT. DRIVEWAY/JACK'S HOUSE - NIGHT (LATER)   49

      The party is coming to a close and people are trying to get
      in their cars and get out of the driveway.

      CAMERA hangs with Little Bill and his Wife.

                         LITTLE BILL
               Thanks for fucking up this party for me.
               I appreciate it.

                         LITTLE BILL'S WIFE
               Oh Fuck Off. Will You?

                         LITTLE BILL
               You Fuck Off.

                         LITTLE BILL'S WIFE
               Yeah, right.

CAMERA MOVES TO FIND: THE YOUNG STUD AND THE LIMO DRIVER.
They're sitting by the limo. The Young Stud is crying.

                    LIMO DRIVER
              Hey, hey, hey. I mean: How were
              you supposed to know?

                    YOUNG STUD
              I wasn't.

                    LIMO DRIVER
              That's right. So what did you do wrong?

                    YOUNG STUD
              Nothing?

                    LIMO DRIVER
              Nothing is absolutely right, Young Stud.

                    YOUNG STUD
              Thank you for your help.

                    LIMO DRIVER
              No problem.

The Colonel and Jack approach. The Colonel now has ANOTHER
YOUNG LADY FRIEND, picked up from the party.

                    COLONEL
              You ready, Johnny?

                    LIMO DRIVER
              Yes, sir.

                    COLONEL
              How you doin' pal?

                    YOUNG STUD
              I'm okay, sir.

                    COLONEL
              Don't worry about it. She'll be fine.

                    YOUNG STUD
              She died in the limo on the way to the hospital.

                    COLONEL
              I didn't hear that.

                    YOUNG STUD
              What?

                    COLONEL
              You never told me that and what happened,
              never happened. You get me?

                              YOUNG STUD
                    I get you.

                              COLONEL
                    Now go home. Sleep it off.

          The Young Stud exits.

                              JACK
                    Thanks for coming, Colonel.

                              COLONEL
                    Great party, Jack.

          The Colonel and the new Lady Friend get in the car.

                                                  CUT TO:

50   EXT. JACK'S HOUSE/POOL AREA - NIGHT (LATER)   50

          The party is over. Amber and Rollergirl are inside playing cards.
          Scotty J. is cleaning up, Dirk and Reed sit in the JACUZZI, looking up
          at the stars.

                              REED
                    ...you wanna hear a poem I wrote?

                              DIRK
                    Yeah.

                              REED
                    Okay. Um...
                    "I love you. You love me.
                    Going down the Sugar Tree.
                    We'll go down the Sugar Tree.
                    And See Lots of Bees. Playing.
                    Playing. The bees won't sting.
                    'Cause you love me."

                              DIRK
                    That's fucking great, man.

          Jack approaches in a bath robe, holding a towel.

                              JACK
                    Howdy-boys.

                              DIRK/REED
                    Hey, Jack.

          Jack removes his robe and climbs in the Jacuzzi.

                              JACK
                    Good party?

                              DIRK
                    It was great.

                    JACK
Good. You had a good time then?

                    DIRK
Excellent time. Thank you.

                    JACK
What this place is for, right?

                    REED
Right.

                    JACK
Ahhhh....this feels good. Bubbles.
Turn those bubbles higher, Reed.

                    DIRK
Jack...I was thinking about my name...y'know...?

                    JACK
Yeah?

                    DIRK
I was wondering if you had any ideas.

                    JACK
I've got a few...but you tell me...

                    DIRK
Well...my idea was...y'know...
I want a name...I want it so it
can cut glass...y'know...razer sharp.

                    JACK
Tell me.

                    DIRK
When I close my eyes...I see this thing,
a sign...I see this name in bright blue neon
lights with a purple outline. And this name
is so bright and so sharp that the sign --
it just blows up because the name is so powerful...

                                        FLASH ON:

A BRIGHT NEON SIGN IN BLUE LETTERING, WITH A PURPLE OUTLINE:

                DIRK DIGGLER

                    DIRK (OC)
It says, "Dirk Diggler."

The NEON SIGNS FLASHES, BUZZES, THEN BURSTS INTO AN ELECTRIC FLAME.

                                        BACK TO:

51   EXT. JACUZZI - THAT MOMENT   51

      Back to Reed and Jack. They look at Dirk.

                          JACK
                Heaven sent you here to this place,
                Dirk Diggler. You've been blessed.

      Dirk smiles. Reed smiles. Jack looks up and closes his eyes.

                                        FADE OUT, CUT TO:

52   INT. JACK'S GARAGE/FILM STUDIO - DAY   52

      ....The film crew sets up lights and other equipment around
      a small "office" set. The crew consists of; Kurt Longjohn, Director
      of Photography. Rocky, Gaffer/Grip. Little Bill, Assistant Director.
      Scotty J. is working as a utility/sound man.

      Jack is sipping coffee, confering with Kurt about lighting.

                          JACK
                How close?

                          KURT LONGJOHN
                Give me twenty to thirty. I've got a
                couple tough shadows to deal with --

                          JACK
                Okay, but not too long, Kurt, right?
                Remember: there are shadows in real life.

      Little Bill approaches.

                          LITTLE BILL
                You wanna go over this?

                          JACK
                Yeah. Let's....

                          LITTLE BILL
                     (reading from script)
                Okay. Set up is....here we go:
                1.) Amber talking to Becky about auditions.
                They make the phone call to the agency to
                send over some actors.
                2.) Enter Reed to audition for Amber.
                They go at it. Becky just watches.
                C.) Becky goes to the bathroom to jack-off
                and is interrupted by Amber. They get into it.
                E.) Enter Dirk --
                     (looks up)
                Who's Dirk Diggler?

                          JACK
                The kid, Eddie, from the club.

                    LITTLE BILL
          Good name. Anyway: 4.) Dirk enters.
          Meets with Becky. They go at it --

                    JACK
          I wanna change that -- that should be Amber.
          Dirk should be auditioning with Amber.

Little Bill makes a note. Jack walks over to Becky, who's
sitting in a chair, shaving her pubic hairs.

                    JACK
          Becky, honey --

                    BECKY
          What?

                    JACK
          What're you doing? We're shooting
          in twenty minutes.

                    BECKY
          I'm shaving my bush --

                    JACK
          Now?

                    BECKY
          It only takes two seconds, Jack.

                    JACK
          Fine, fine.

Jack continues to get everyone ready.

                    JACK
          Alright everyone, let's go, let's go,
          we need to shoot this first scene --
          we need to get one off --

                                        CUT TO:

53   INT. BEDROOM - DAY - LATER   53

Dirk is sitting on the edge of the bed, dressed up in a brown suit and
his hair is brushed back, parted down the middle. He paces a little,
does some deep breathing, looks over script, etc. Scotty J. enters.

                    SCOTTY J.
          Hey. Hi. Dirk. Dirk Diggler.

                    DIRK
          Hi.

                    SCOTTY J.
          I'm supposed to come get you.
          Tell you they're ready, now.

                    DIRK
Okay.

                    SCOTTY J.
You look really good.

                    DIRK
Thank you.

                    SCOTTY J.
You look really sexy.

                    DIRK
Thanks.

                    SCOTTY J.
I like your name.

                    DIRK
You do?

                    SCOTTY J.
It's really cool.

                    DIRK
Thanks.

                    SCOTTY J.
OK...well...whenever you're ready....
I'll see you out there.

Scotty J. exits. Dirk stands, takes a deep breath. CAMERA follows
as he exits the room and walks through the house and into --

54   INT. GARAGE/FILM SET   54
the crew is ready and waiting. Jack is there to greet him.

                    JACK
Ready, champ?

                    DIRK
Let's do this.

They walk through the scene with Amber.

                    JACK
So we know the scene, we know the thing.
You're gonna start outside the set,
through that door, I'll call your name
and action, that'll be your cue...come through
the door, straight to the desk, right here,
boom, you and Amber do the scene --

                    DIRK
Do we go straight into having sex?

                    JACK
          Is that alright?

                    DIRK
          It would be better I think, y'know,
          so we don't break up the momentum
          or something --

                    JACK
          Amber?

                    AMBER
          Good.

                    JACK
          So we'll just go straight through.

                    DIRK
          Okay.

                    KURT LONGJOHN
          Are we doing a rehersal?

                    JACK
          Eddie, you want a rehersal?

                    DIRK
          It's okay...I can do it...

                    JACK
          Great.

                    DIRK
          Jack?

                    JACK
          Yeah?

                    DIRK
          ...can you...um...will you call me
          Dirk Diggler from now on?

                    JACK
          Yes. I'm sorry, yeah, yes.

     Jack exits. Amber and Dirk huddle in the corner a moment.

                    AMBER
          Do you want to practice your lines with me.

                    DIRK
          I know it.

                    AMBER
          You look great, honey.

                    DIRK
Does he want me to keep going until I come?

                    AMBER
Yeah. You just come when you're ready....

                    DIRK
Where should I come?

                    AMBER
Where do you want?

                    DIRK
Wherever you tell me.

                    AMBER
Come on my tits if you can, okay?
Just pull it out and do it on
my stomach and tits if you can.

                    DIRK
Yeah.

She touches her hand softly to the side of his face. (30fps)

                    AMBER
Are you alright, honey?

                    DIRK
This is great. I'm ready. I wanna do good.
I wanna do this good....let's try and do it
really sexy...you want to?

                    AMBER
Okay.

Little Bill takes Dirk and walks him off the set, explaining
things one last time to him....CAMERA HOLDS ON DIRK. Little
Bill walks away and he's left standing alone a moment, waiting
for his cue behind a closed door. SILENCE. HOLD.

                    JACK (OC)
and....action, Dirk.

CAMERA blends to SLOW MOTION (30fps) and FOLLOWS Dirk through
the door and into the set -- lights flare into CAMERA/DIRK and
we focus in on Amber, seated behind a desk. CAMERA blends back
to 24fps.

KURT LONGJOHN'S 16mm CAMERA POV:
Dirk enters. A light shines straight at him. He walks
into a two shot with Amber at the desk. BEAT, THEN:

                    AMBER
Hello. Are you John?

                    DIRK
    Yes, ma'am.

                    AMBER
    Your agency recommends you very highly.

                    DIRK
    I'm a really hard worker. You give
    me a job and I won't disappoint you.

                    AMBER
    What special skills do you have?

                    DIRK
    Well, I spent three years in the Marines.
    I just got back from a tour of duty.

                    AMBER
    You're kidding?

                    DIRK
    No I'm not. It got really hard being
    surrounded by guys all day.

                    AMBER
    When was the last time you had a woman?

                    DIRK
    A long time.

                    AMBER
    That's terrible.

                    DIRK
    But I'm back now and I'm ready to pursue
    my acting career.

                    AMBER
    Well as you may or may not know, this is an
    important film for me. If it's not a hit,
    I'm gonna get kicked out of my apartment.
    My landlord is a real jerk.

                    DIRK
    Really?

                    AMBER
    Why don't you take your pants off?
    It's important that I get an idea of your size.

                    DIRK
    No problem.

    Dirk starts to remove his pants...just before they come off we go to:

JACK AND THE REST OF THE CREW
Kurt Longjohn takes his eye away from the viewfinder for a moment.
Rocky frowns slightly. Scotty J. is in shock. Reed and Becky smile.

Amber looks from Dirk's cock to his face.

                    AMBER
          I think that you have the part,
          but why don't I make sure of something...

16mm CAMERA'S POV:
for the first time, we see Dirk's cock. It hangs about 12 inches.
Amber's hand reaches and grabs hold of it --

                    AMBER
          This is a giant cock.

So they go at it...taking each other's clothes off and climbing
up on the desk...OUR CAMERA is hand held, moving around, looking
at the crew filming and Dirk/Amber making love....

They continue for a while. Jack whispers something to Kurt,
then walks over to Dirk and Amber, quietly interupts;

                    JACK
          Guys...

                    DIRK
          Is everything cool?

                    JACK
          Hang in there, everything's cool,
          I just wanna change the angle --
          You're doin' great.

Amber looks to Dirk. They holds still;

                    AMBER
          You're doin' so good, Dirk.

                    DIRK
          Does it feel good?

Amber smiles. Jack and Kurt have set up a new angle;

                    JACK
          Okay -- we're back, we're ready -- action --

They continue for a bit, getting faster and a little harder;

CU. DIRK AND AMBER.
they're face to face. Following in sotto:

                    AMBER
          You're amazing.

                    DIRK
          You feel good, Amber.

                    AMBER
          Are you ready to come?

                    DIRK
          Yes.

                    AMBER
          Come in me.

                    DIRK
          What?

                    AMBER
          Don't worry, I'm fixed.
          I want you to come in me --

Amber and Dirk come together. HOLD. They kiss and smile.

                    JACK
          CUT! FUCK! YES! YES! YES!

THE CREW APPLAUDS THE PERFORMANCE. Everyone gathers around.
Dirk is giving hand shakes, high fives, etc.

CAMERA PANS over to Little Bill and Jack who step aside a moment.
Following in sotto;

                    JACK
          That was great.

                    LITTLE BILL
          Yes it was. What do you want to
          do about the come shot? We could
          go to the stock footage -- get a close up --

                    JACK
          It's not gonna match, we don't
          have a cock that big on film --

Dirk hears this and turns to Jack and Little Bill.

                    DIRK
          Jack?

                    JACK
          Yes, Dirk?

                    DIRK
          I can do it again if you need a close-up.

Everyone in the room looks at Dirk. HOLD.

MUSIC CUE. CONTINUES OVER CUT AND THE FOLLOWING SCENES:

55   INT. JACK'S LIVING ROOM - NIGHT - LATER   Sequence "A"   55

The entire cast and crew together.

ECU - CHAMPAGNE BOTTLES POP

ECU - ROLLERGIRL'S CAMERA.
she snaps POLAROIDS.

ECU - DEVELOPED PICTURES
cast and crew smiling, holding thumbs up. Dirk in the middle.

                                      CUT TO:

56   INT. RESEDA SHOE STORE - DAY   56

CAMERA TRACKS ALONG a row of shoes. Dirk, Reed and Scotty J.
in the store, picking some out. Dirk falls in love with a pair of
half-boots, zip-up style --

                                      CUT TO:

57   INT. HOT TRAXX NIGHTCLUB - NIGHT   57

CAMERA BEGINS ON THE SHOES, DOES A QUICK BOOM UP TO A CU.
ON DIRK. He's dancing with Rollergirl. They talk about his shoes.

                            QUICK DISSOLVE TO:

OVERHEAD ANGLE, JACK'S TABLE.
Jack is eating Clams On The Half Shell and talking to Amber.
The Colonel is sitting with a NEW LADY FRIEND. CAMERA begins
a BOOM DOWN as Scotty J. enters FRAME and begins talking the
Colonel's ear off.

                            QUICK DISSOLVE TO:

ANGLE, MAURICE
CAMERA follows behind him as he shouts orders to waiters
and busboys and bouncers --

                            QUICK DISSOLVE TO:

ANGLE, BECKY
She's hanging out near the bathroom with a GIRLFRIEND and
flirting with some YOUNG GENT, who's a body-builder-type.

                            QUICK DISSOLVE TO:

INSIDE THE DJ BOOTH. A couple young girls surround the DJ,
who is a BLACK MIDGET, wearing headphones, dancing and doing
coke with the girls. He sets up another RECORD on the turntable.
CAMERA DOLLIES IN QUICK ON THE RECORD, NEW MUSIC CUE.

                                    CUT TO:

58   INT. MOTEL ROOM FILM SET - ANOTHER DAY   58

    Cast and Crew shooting a new film with a Spanish-theme. Jack watches
    Rollergirl and Dirk who are on a WATERBED. They block the scene.

                   JACK
          What we can do is make it all one thing, right?
          You can go from being on top -- below and then
          move and shift to the side -- pump away
          there for a while, then --

    Dirk gets on the bed with Rollergirl and tries a move.

                   DIRK
          If she...Rollergirl...if you wrap your leg
          around...other one...your left leg....right...
          up around my neck. And over. Good.
          We can go right into Doggy Style.

                 KURT LONGJOHN
          Is the movement of the waterbed a problem?

                   DIRK
          Not at all, Kurt. Matter of fact, I dig it.

                                 CUT TO:

59   OMITTED ** Director's Note: 2nd Unit/TBA   59 *

                              BURN TO:

60   INT. JACK'S HOUSE/KITCHEN - DAY   60

    Jack is reading, "Oui." Dirk, Reed and Amber listen;

                   JACK
          Jack Horner has found something special
          in new-comer, Dirk Diggler. It's another
          stellar, sexual standout from Horner and Company.
          Diggler delivers a performance worth a thousand
          hard-ons. His presence when dressed is powerful
          and demanding....

    CAMERA DOLLIES IN ON THE PAGE, TRACKS ALONG THE WORDS.
    CAMERA catches glimpses of the words on the page, "...Diggler..."
    "...sexual standout..." "...supple ass...." Continue w/STILL
    PHOTOGRAPHS from the film.

                          SPLIT SCREEN TO:

61   INT. STUDIO CITY HAIR SALON - DAY   61

      CAMERA DOLLIES DOWN THE LINE OF HAIRSTYLISTS. Dirk is getting
      a fluffy new hair style. Reed stands nearby and watches;

                          JACK (VO)
                ...when stripped to the bone, Diggler's
                more eruptive than a volcano on a bad day.
                Amber Waves ripe-cherry lips do a wonderful
                job of handling Diggler's wide load and
                Reed Rothchild's stiff biceps do a slapping
                good job with Becky Barnett's supple ass...

                                    THREE-WAY SPLIT TO:

62   A CLIP FROM THE FILM, "SPANISH PANTALONES." (16mm)   62

      This is filmed on the Motel Room Film Set. Reed is wearing speedos
      and a sombrero. Becky is naked. He slaps her ass. Dirk is facing
      CAMERA, Amber is kneeling down, covering his crotch giving him
      a blow job. CU. Dirk for the money shot.

                                    FOUR WAY SPLIT TO:

63   INT. HOT TRAXX NIGHTCLUB - NIGHT   63

      Dirk is disco dancing with Rollergirl and Becky and Reed.

                          JACK (VO)
                ...but it's Diggler that remains the standout
                in this film. It's easy to predict, after only
                two films, that Diggler's suck-cess can only grow
                and grow and grow --

      END FOUR WAY SPLIT, STAYING WITH DIRK DANCING IN THE CLUB.
      Dirk, Reed, Rollergirl, Buck, Maurice and Becky begin doing
      a DANCE NUMBER. (Complete w/coreographed moves, etc.)

                                    CUT TO:

64   OMITTED   64

65   INT. JACK'S HOUSE/AMBER'S BEDROOM - NIGHT   65

      Amber is on the phone. Dirk is sitting with her, holding her hand.

                          AMBER
                Please let me talk to him, Tom.
                Please. I just want to say hello
                and that's all -- I'm not. I'm completely sober.
                I'm not -- Tom -- Tom -- Tom --

      Dial tone from the phone, she hangs up --

                          AMBER
                I don't know what to do now.

                                              CUT TO:

66   INT. HOT TRAXX NIGHTCLUB/BACKROOM - DAY   66

      Maurice slips a PHOTOGRAPH and a letter into an envelope and seals it
      up. The VO is in Spanish, with SUB-TITLES.

                         MAURICE (VO)
                Dear brothers: I'm sending you a picture --

                                              CUT TO:

67   INT. APARTMENT BLDG./PUERTO RICO - DAY   67 *

      Maurice's two BROTHERS rip open the letter and check out a picture of *
      Maurice standing next to Rollergirl.

                         MAURICE (VO)
                -- this is my girlfriend. I had sex
                with her last night. Isn't she hot?
                I get chicks like this every night.

                                              CUT TO:

68   OMITTED   68 *

69   INT. KARATE STUDIO - DAY   69

      Buck, Dirk and Reed dressed in Karate-gear, are taking lessons.
      Buck speaks about the ancient history of Karate.

                                              CUT TO:

70   INT. DEPARTMENT STORE - DAY   70

      CAMERA TRACKS ALONG A ROW OF SUITS. Dirk picks one out, tries
      it on and pays for it in cash. CAMERA then PUSHES IN through a
      series of QUICK DISSOLVES on SUITS hanging individually on the wall.

                                              CUT TO:

71   OMITTED   71

72   EXT. DESERT HIGHWAY - DAY   72

      CAMERA moves with Jack's Big Van and Little Bill's Station Wagon that *
      follows.   *

                                              CUT TO:

<u>INT. JACK'S VAN - MOVING - DAY</u> (music over into radio)

  Amber is driving the van, Buck is in the passenger seat trying
  to figure out why the radio isn't working and speaking;

        BUCK
    If you were to open a bussiness
    specializing in, like, Super-Super
    Hi-Fi Stereo Equipment -- forget it,
    you're in the money. I mean, there's
    no limit to the technology that's
    comin' out now --

        AMBER
    Really?

        BUCK
    That's a fact.

        AMBER
    So what's wrong with this radio?

        BUCK
    I think it's...uh...it's a wattage
    problem...yeah...we've got to many
    watts per channel going into the
    front two speakers....yeah...

  IN THE BACK OF THE VAN:
  Reed, Dirk and Jack are huddled, speaking intensely;

        JACK
    -- what else?

        DIRK
    That's it for now. I mean: I look
    at this character Holmes has come
    up with -- and -- look -- I just --

        JACK
    Tell me.

        DIRK
    I don't like to see women treated that way.
    This guy he plays, "Johnny Wad," it's always
    about slapping some girl around or whatever.
    It's not right, it's not cool and it just...
    isn't sexy. It isn't <u>sexy</u> like it should be.

        REED
    We could make it more of a James Bond
    character. This guy that's world traveled.

        JACK
    I like that.

                    DIRK
          Reed could play my partner.

                    JACK
          I like this a lot.

                    DIRK
          We could make it really good, Jack.
          Honestly. If you direct it...we could
          make a whole series, with a whole story.
          This is exactly what we've always talked about.

                    JACK
          I know it. I know it.

                    REED
          We should do this.

                    JACK
          Alright. When we get back. We'll set up
          the typewriter and we'll see what we can
          come up with. I'll talk to the Colonel when
          we get to Vegas. But Dirk, you gotta work
          on him too, okay?

                    DIRK
          Right, right.

                    JACK
          -- if we don't put every element into this,
          it's just not gonna work...

                    DIRK
          Exactly.

                    JACK
          Now: What's this guy's name?
          This character? Do you know?

                    DIRK
          His name is Brock Landers.

                    REED
          His partner's name is Chest Rockwell.

                    JACK
          ....those are great names.

                                        CUT TO:

74   OMITTED   74 *

75   INT. ALADDIN HOTEL/CASINO - BANQUET ROOM - NIGHT   75

       The "2nd ANNUAL ADULT FILM AWARDS." Behind a small PODIUM and
       in front of a packed to capacity CROWD of porn filmmakers is --

       AMBER. She's about to open an envelope.

                              AMBER
                  And the award for, "Best NewComer,"
                  goes to....Yes! My baby-boy...DIRK DIGGLER!

                                                        JUMP CUT TO:

       COLONEL JAMES. He's on stage, rips open an envelope.

                           COLONEL JAMES
                  ...the award for, "Best Cock,"
                  goes to...Here We Go Again...DIRK DIGGLER.

                                                        JUMP CUT TO:

       A Porn Actress, JESSIE ST. VINCENT (early 20s) She opens;

                              JESSIE
                  And The Award...for Best Actor Goes To....
                  I've seen his movies and I can't wait to
                  work with him, I can't wait to get that big
                  cock in my mouth, my ass, my pussy or any
                  which way he'll give it to me....Mr. Dirk Diggler!

       The Audience Applauds wildly. Dirk, dressed in a jean outfit,
       makes his way to the stage and accepts the award from Jessie.
       He turns to the crowd.

DIRK
Wow. I dunno what to say....I guess. Wow.
I guess the only thing I can say, is that
I promise to keep rocking and rolling and
to keep making better films. It seems we make
these movies...and sometimes...they're considered
filthy or something by some people...but I don't
think that's true. These films we make can be
better...they can help...they really can, I mean it.
We can always do better -- and I'll keep trying
if you keep trying so let's keep ROCKING AND ROLLING.

AUDICENCE APPLAUDS. Jessie St. Vincent comes over and plants
a deep, wet kiss right in his mouth;

JESSIE ST. VINCENT
You're hot.

Amber, in the audience, sees the kiss and frowns. Dirk raises
the award high above his head and does a karate move --

CUT TO:

76   INT. ITALIAN RESTARAUNT SET - DAY   (16mm)   Sequence "B"   76 *

TITLE CARD READS: "1978"

*

...Jessie St. Vincent walks across the restaurant to the bar.
Kurt Longjohn and his camera crew track with her. Dirk, in character
with his hair slicked, chewing on a toothpick and smoking a cigarette,
wearing a suit and sunglasses is sitting at the bar. She speaks to
the Bartender (played by Maurice.)

JESSIE ST. VINCENT
Shot of Tequila, straight up.

MAURICE
Yes, ma'am.

JESSIE ST. VINCENT
(to Dirk)
I've been in this place twenty minutes,
just to get a seat.

DIRK
You alone?

JESSIE ST. VINCENT
Yeah. Just visiting L.A. Some people
told me the food in here was really good.

                    DIRK
          Good. No it's not good. It's probably
          the BEST place to eat in Los Angeles.
          It's excellent.

                    JESSIE ST. VINCET
          I certainly hope so. I could die of
          starvation before I get something in my mouth --

                                                    JUMP CUT TO:

77   INT. BEDROOM SET - NIGHT - SCENE CONTINUED IN CLIP FORM. (16mm)   77

      This bedroom set is decorated as Brock Landers pad.
      Jessie St. Vincent unzips Dirk's pants...(porn music in b.g.)

                    DIRK
          You said you were hungry --

                    JESSIE ST. VINCENT
          Starving.

                    DIRK
          Well, go ahead and feast.

      She pulls his cock out of his fly, looks at it. CAMERA sees this.

                    JESSIE ST. VINCENT
          ohhh. It's true --

                    DIRK
          What?

                    JESSIE ST. VINCENT
          You're Brock Landers --

                                                    CUT TO:

78   EXT. VARIOUS VALLEY LOCATIONS - DAY - FILM CLIP (16mm)   78

      TITLE SEQUENCE FROM; "Brock Landers: Angels Live In My Town."
      Dirk is running STRAIGHT TOWARDS CAMERA in a JEAN OUTFIT.
      He stops, does a KARATE KICK and turns -- FREEZE FRAME.

      TITLE READS: DIRK DIGGLER as BROCK LANDERS

      Various other footage of Reed, running down the street, firing
      a gun and knocking people down. FREEZE FRAME.

      TITLE READS: REED ROTHCHILD as CHEST ROCKWELL.

      Finally, over a WIDE ANGLE SHOT OF VENTURA BLVD;

                "BROCK LANDERS: ANGELS LIVE IN MY TOWN"

                                                    MATCH CUT TO:

INT. JACK'S HOUSE - EDITING ROOM - DAY   79

CAMERA PULLS BACK and WHIPS around from the Steenbeck image
to find; Jack and Kurt Longjohn, working on the film.

                    JACK
          Good, good, it's close. Let's head trim
          Dirk's spin, loose Reed with the revolver
          and switch the main title card -- it should
          really fly towards camera --

                                              CUT TO:

80   INT. DIRK'S NEW HOUSE/STUDIO CITY HILLS - DAY   80

CAMERA (STEADICAM) begins on Reed who's doing a MAGIC TRICK
in the living room for Scotty J. and Becky. Jessie is oil painting.

Dirk and Amber enter FRAME and CAMERA follows them through the
house. Dirk is giving her a tour, explaining what type of
leather couches he has, what sort of history he knows about the
wood used to build the house, showing her a painting on the wall
of himself that was done by Jessie St. Vincent, etc. They move into --

THE KITCHEN
Maurice and Rollergirl are deep in conversation. He's trying
to convince her that she should take a picture with him without
her clothes on so he can send it to his brothers in Puerto Rico.

CAMERA stays foreground with their conversation while Dirk
shows Amber the back deck area of the house --
(Director's Note: Sound covers the four talking simultaneously.)

Rollergirl stops arguing with Maurice;

                    ROLLERGIRL
          Fuck it, fine, let's go.

She rips off her bikini top, sets the POLAROID on the counter,
hits the timer, rolls back and poses with Maurice --

CU - DEVELOPED POLAROID
the image is of their waists - the Polaroid framing was too low.

Dirk and Amber come f.g. and CAMERA leads them --

                    DIRK
          And around this corner is the big surprise.
          The main thing I wanna show you --

The move down a hallway and into --

THE GARAGE
it's dark for a moment, Dirk hits the garage door and it starts
to open...LIGHT POURS INSIDE on their faces --

                    DIRK
              Isn't it beautiful?

CAMERA holds CU images of a BRAND NEW 1978 CORVETTE. It's candy apple
.red with super trimmed out designs, etc. CAMERA DOLLIES IN ON DIRK.

                    AMBER
              You deserve this, baby.

                    DIRK
              This is it -- this is the thing.
              This is the most beautiful thing
              I've ever seen in my life --

They get in the car and go for a ride.

                                                    CUT TO:

81   INT. ITALIAN RESTARAUNT SET - NIGHT - FILM CLIP (16mm)   81

Dirk and Reed, in charachter look at each other and say;

                    DIRK
              So we solved the case and the women
              are safe --

                    REED
              Just another day.

                    DIRK
              That's right.

                    REED
              C'mon, Brock. Let's go out and get
              some of that Saturday Night Beaver --

They smile. FREEZE FRAME. TITLE CARD READS: Directed By Jack Horner

                                          MATCH CUT TO:

82   INT. JACK'S HOUSE - EDITING ROOM - DAY   82

CAMERA PULLS BACK and WHIPS around from the Steenbeck image
to find Jack and Kurt Longjohn;

                    JACK
              This is the best work I've ever done.

                    KURT
              It's a real film, Jack.

                         JACK
           It feels good.

                         KURT
           You made it fly.

                         JACK
           This is the one they'll remember me by, baby.

                                                CUT TO:

83   OMITTED ** Director's Note: 2nd Unit/TBA   83 *

                                          QUICK DISSOLVE TO:

84   OMITTED ** Director's Note: 2nd Unit/TBA   84 *

                                          QUICK DISSOLVE TO:

85   OMITTED ** Director's Note: 2nd Unit/TBA   85 *

                                             BURN WHITE TO:

86   INT. ALADDIN BANQUET ROOM - NIGHT   86

     The "4th ANNUAL ADULT FILM AWARDS." Dirk walks up to the podium
     to accept another award.

     CAMERA DOLLIES IN ON EACH OF OUR PRINCIPLES SO FAR IN SLOW MOTION:
     Reed. Jack. Amber. Little Bill...then PAN to his Wife.
     Kurt Longjohn. Rocky. Becky. Jessie St. Vincent. Scotty J.
     Maurice. Buck. Colonel and another new Lady Friend. Rollergirl.
     Finally, Dirk. He speaks into the microphone;

                         DIRK
           Thank you.

     FREEZE FRAME ON DIRK. End Sequence "B"
                                                WIPE TO:

INT. JACK'S HOUSE - NIGHT

CAMERA starts on a huge banner strung across the house. It reads:

          "Goodbye 70's -- Hello 80's"

CAMERA roams through the party. This is a bigger, better and more insane party than we have seen so far....

CAMERA hangs with Becky and a tall, heavy-set black guy JEROME.

                    BECKY
          ...right, right...

                    JEROME
          yeah....y'know....as far as I'm concerned,
          it's about love. Y'know? You love someone
          and how hard can the world be? I mean,
          people will come and go and so will problems,
          and ultimately, if you have love on your side
          and in your soul, whatsa problem gonna be
          that takes your attention away? Y'understand?

                    BECKY
          I do...I do. That's really sweet.

                    JEROME
          My name's Jerome.

                    BECKY
          I'm Becky.

                    JEROME
          Nice to meet 'ya, Becky.

                    BECKY
          What do you do?

                    JEROME
          I'm in the auto industry.

                    BECKY
          Really?

                    JEROME
          Yeah. I'm regional manager
          for "Pep Boys."

                    BECKY
          That's great.

                    JEROME
          You've got a nice smile, Becky.

                    BECKY
          Thank you.

CAMERA hangs with Kurt and Rocky who are discussing technology and the future....

CAMERA hangs with Reed, who's doing some Magic Tricks for Jack and explaining some facts about, "the world of illusions."

CAMERA hangs with Dirk and Jessie St. Vincent.

                    JESSIE ST. VINCENT
          Because sometimes I feel like an outsider
          to the whole thing. Y'know...I see you and
          Amber and your relationship and I dunno --

                    DIRK
          No, no, Jessie. You shouldn't feel
          like an outsider.

                    JESSIE ST. VINCENT
          I know my tits aren't as big and I know
          my pussy isn't as tight as all the other
          girls in this industry but I still feel
          like I've got something that works --
          I can paint, too.

                    DIRK
          Yes. Yes. Yes.

                    JESSIE ST. VINCENT
          I dunno. I was just never really secure.
          When I was a kid, I was never really secure
          with myself that much -- I guess that's why
          I try and act like I'm all care-free and everything.

                    DIRK
          I know what you mean, sometimes I'm like,
          "What am I doing?" "What the hell is wrong
          with me?" Y'know?

                    JESSIE ST. VINCENT
          I know, I know.

                    DIRK
          But then...I think...

                    JESSIE ST. VINCENT
          -- it's just fun. It's great.

                    DIRK
          It is. It's the best. I mean, look:
          I couldn't be happier than where
          I am today, right now, at this moment.

                    JESSIE ST. VINCENT
          You are so fucking awesome, Dirk.

DIRK
Who says you don't have a tight pussy?

JESSIE ST. VINCENT
I don't know. No one, I guess.

CAMERA hangs with Scotty J. and Amber. He re-counts;

SCOTTY J.
So I was all, "What's your problem?"
And he was all, "Nothing." So I was
like...really...y'know...I was fuckin'
pissed, Amber. So then I was all,
like, "What are you gonna do?" Y'know?
And he was all, like acting tough,
y'know, with his friends around and stuff.
So I was just all...like..."Forget it."
And I walked away.

Amber's attention moves to Dirk talking with Jessie St. Vincent.

AMBER
Excuse me, Scotty.

CUT TO:

88   INT. JACK'S HOUSE/KITCHEN - NIGHT   88

CAMERA hangs with The Colonel, a NEW LADY FRIEND, who's doing some
coke from a bowl and Maurice, who's begging for a part in a movie.
The Colonel's attention turns across the room;

COLONEL'S POV: A tall man in a white suite, FLOYD GONDOLLI (mid 50s)
is standing with two dirty-looking BOYS and two similar GIRLS.

The Colonel walks over, CAMERA WHIP PANS over to Floyd Gondolli;

FLOYD
The Colonel!

COLONEL
Floyd Gondolli, great you could make
it...great...great...great.

FLOYD
How are you? You look happy.

COLONEL
I'm fine.

FLOYD
Meet Boys: Tommy and Pete.
Meet Girls: Angie and Cyndi.

TOMMY/PETE/ANGIE/CYNDI
Hi.

                    COLONEL
        Hello. Happy New Year.

                    FLOYD
        These are the next stars...the real
        people in the world.

                    COLONEL
        I think we should do that talk with
        Jack now, whadda 'ya say? Maybe iron
        this thing out before we start the new year...   *

                    FLOYD
        Let's do it.

Floyd turns to the kids he is with and speaks very slowly to them;

                    FLOYD
        Tommy-Pete-Angie-Cyndi. Uncle Floyd is gonna
        split for a minute to do a little business talk.

The Colonel and Floyd walk away.

                                        CUT TO:

89   EXT. POOL AREA - NIGHT - THAT MOMENT   89

Dirk is talking with Jessie St. Vincent. Amber comes over and
takes a seat on Dirk's lap.

                    DIRK
        Hey, Amber.

                    AMBER
        What are you talking about out here?

                    DIRK
        Nothin'

                    AMBER
        Do you wanna come with me for a little while?

                    DIRK
        Where?

                    AMBER
        A surprise, surprise, surprise.

                    DIRK
        Let's go.

They excuse themselves from Jessie and walk off into the house.
Jessie looks across the party and sees Buck. CAMERA moves away,
towards him --

He's sitting alone, wearing a new-style, Commodores look.
A few beats later -- Jessie enters frame.

              JESSIE
      Hey, Buck.

              BUCK
      Hey, Jessie, how ya doin'?

              JESSIE
      You sitting alone?

                           CUT TO:

90   EXT. JACK'S DRIVEWAY - NIGHT - THAT MOMENT   90

A guy in white jeans, black leather jacket, TODD PARKER (late 20s.)
He exits his 280z and flashes smiles at various party people.
CAMERA follows him to the POOL AREA where he sees;

              REED
      Todd Parker.

              TODD
      Rockin' Reed Rothchild.

              REED
      You made it --

                         TODD
              Yeah...yeah. This is an amazing party.
              Fuckin' chicks everywhere.

                         REED
              You bet.

                         TODD
              I wouldn't mind havin' some of that
              action over there --

Todd points out a BIKINI PARTY GIRL.

                         REED
              Want me to introduce you?

                         TODD
              Sure. Introduce her to my lap.

                         REED
              You got off work?

                         TODD
              I don't dance Sunday nights.
              Who's Corvette is that out in the driveway?

                         REED
              It's Dirk's.

                         TODD
              That car is jammin' -- Nosed, Racked,
              Dual Camms, Ten Coats of Hand Gloss,
              Candy Apple Red Laquer - WHOA.

                                              CUT TO:

90A   EXT. POOL AREA - THAT MOMENT   90A *

       Buck and Jessie St. Vincent sitting/talking.   *

                         BUCK   *
              I'm pretty happy with it...   *

                         JESSIE ST. VINCENT   *
              ...It's a great look for you, I think.   *

                         BUCK   *
              It's sort of original, I think.   *

                         JESSIE ST. VINCENT   *
              Right.   *

                         BUCK   *
              What were we talking about before?   *

                    JESSIE ST. VINCENT
          Um....oil painting...?   *

                         BUCK   *
          No...yes, I mean...but we were talkin'   *
          about...   *

                    JESSIE ST. VINCENT   *
          oh! oh! "Sunsets."   *

                         BUCK   *
          Oh yeah! I was saying: I like sunsets too...but... *

                    JESSIE ST. VINCENT   *
          Sunrises are better.   *

                         BUCK   *
          Exactly.   *

                    JESSIE ST. VINCENT   *
          I thought I was the only one who thought that. *

                         BUCK   *
          I think that.   *

                    JESSIE ST. VINCENT   *
          I never thought we'd have so much   *
          in common, Buck.   *

                         BUCK   *
          Yeah, yeah....hey, have you ever heard   *
          my stereo system?   *

                    JESSIE ST. VINCENT   *
          No.   *

                         BUCK   *
          Y'know I'm thinking of opening my   *
          own business --   *

                    JESSIE ST. VINCENT   *
          Really?   *

                         BUCK   *
          It's my dream. Hi-Fi Stereo Equipment   *
          at a discount price -- it's called,   *
          "Buck's Super Stereo World."   *

                    JESSIE ST. VINCENT   *
          That's a fucking great idea.   *

                                             CUT TO:

91   <u>INT. JACK'S OFFICE - MOMENTS LATER</u>   91

Jack, Floyd Gondolli and the Colonel sitting.

                    FLOYD
          ...so let's talk about the future.
          So let's talk about what video means
          to this industry -- and let's talk
          about how all of us -- not one of us --
          but all of us will profit. I've been doing
          theater work in San Francisco and San Diego
          for as long as you've been doing stag
          and hard-core, Jack.

                    JACK
          I know you're history, Floyd.

                    COLONEL
          No one's doubting your history
          or your credentials, Floyd.

                    FLOYD
Then why the resistance? I mean:
This industry is going to be turned
upside down soon enough --

                    JACK
Then why help it?

                    FLOYD
Why not be prepared? The money comes
from the Colonel, the talent comes from
you Jack. I've got a connection to the
equipment and the mail order distribution,
not to mention those kids I got out there
who are hot-fuck-action to the max.
This is the future. Video tape tells the truth.

                    JACK
I have a stable of actors and actresses.
They're professionals. They're not
a bunch of fucking amateurs. They're
proven box office and they get people
in theaters (where films should be seen)
and they know how to fuck well --

                    FLOYD
That's right, Jack and by that
same token, you're the one with the
power here. The video revolution
is upon us -- and our role is critical.
We have an obligation to use our resources
and talent to help make it fly --

                    JACK
You come in here, at my party, tell me about
this and that -- tell me about the future,
tell me about -- video and amateurs and
all that -- well lemme tell you something now:
I will not shoot films on video and no
I will not loan out my actors who are
under contract to me. Period.

                    FLOYD
Wait a minute, Jack. I'm not a complicated man.
I like cinema. In particular, I like to
see fucking on film. I don't want to win
an Oscar and I don't want to re-invent the
wheel -- I enjoy simple pleasures like butter
in my ass and lollipops in my mouth.
That's me -- call me crazy, call me a pervert,
but this is something that I enjoy. . One other
small thing I want to do in this life is make
a dollar and a cent in this bussiness -- I'm not
trying to hurt you, I'm trying to help you stay
one step ahead of the game --

                    JACK
We're repeating ourselves now, Floyd.

                         COLONEL
          Jack, I think this about cost and future --

                    JACK
The future is as bright as we make it --
it shouldn't be sacrificed for a few dollars
that can be saved shooting on video tape --
if it looks like shit and sounds like shit,
it probably is shit --

                    FLOYD
I think you're one gin past this conversation --

                    JACK
No...no. I'm crystal clear here.

                         COLONEL
          Jack, please understand that this is
          not an argument...this is a fact of --

                    JACK
....What...?

                         COLONEL
          This is not an argument, but a --

                    JACK
What are you saying?

                         COLONEL
          What do you mean, Jack, c'mon --

                    JACK
Are you telling me that you're
working with this shit?

                         COLONEL
          I think that there is a serious case
          to be made for the price and the gamble
          on the whole idea of a home video market --
          Jack: Two, three years from now, everyone's
          gonna be able to walk into their local
          supermarket and buy or a rent a videocassette --

                    JACK
True film fans won't watch that shit.
It doesn't look good and more importantly
it doesn't make sex look sexy.

                         COLONEL
          It doesn't have to look good, Jack.
          Film is just too damn expensive.
          The theaters are already planning
          converting to video projectors.

                    JACK
          I haven't heard that.

                    FLOYD
          It's true.

                    JACK
          We've got ten minutes until the New
          Year and I don't want it to start like this
          so I'm leaving now. We will or we won't
          continue this conversation some other time.

     Jack leaves. Floyd looks to the Colonel. HOLD.

                                        CUT TO:

92   INT. AMBER'S BEDROOM - NIGHT   92

     Dirk and Amber enter. She sits him on the bed.

                    AMBER
          I wanted you...to just..to come
          in and give me a minute so I could
          tell you how much I love you.
          It's gonna be a new year and we're
          gonna start things and do things
          and I want you to know how much I
          really care for you, honey. I care
          for you so much....you're my little baby...

                    DIRK
          Thank you, Amber.

                    AMBER
          You're the best thing in the world
          that's happened to me since my son
          went off...and I just...I love you, honey.

                    DIRK
          I love you too, Amber.

     Amber continues to talk as she sets up more lines of coke --

                    AMBER
          Fucking 1980...y'know? Can you believe it?

                    DIRK
          I can't...it's like...next thing
          we know...it's gonna be 1990, then
          2000...can you imagine?

                    AMBER
          Goodbye to 1979...hello to 1980...
               (handing him a straw)
          Make sure your snort it back quick and hard....

                        DIRK
        ...wh..?

                        AMBER
        Really fast, like this...

She demonstrates. Dirk hesitates a moment, then leans down
and does a line of coke.

                        DIRK
            It burns.

                        AMBER
        It's good, though, right?

                        DIRK
        It's in my throat....uch...

                        AMBER
        It's the drip...the drip's the best part.

                        DIRK
        Tastes like aspirin.

                        AMBER
        Do one more in the other nostril.

                        DIRK
        ...I need a glass of water, I think...

                        AMBER
        One more, then the water.

Dirk does another line.

                        DIRK
        Do I look cool when I do it?

Amber is right there to KISS him very hard on the mouth. HOLD.

                                                    CUT TO:

93   INT. JACK'S HALLWAY - THAT MOMENT   93

Dirk and Amber emerge from the bedroom and walk back to the
party....Amber stops to say hello to some people....Dirk keeps
walking....CAMERA follows him outside...Scotty J. approaches....

                        SCOTTY J.
        Hey, Dirk.

                        DIRK
        Scotty. Hey. What's up, man?

                        SCOTTY J.
        ...fuckin' New Years, y'know, right?

                    DIRK
        1980.

                    SCOTTY J.
        Right. Did you see my new car?

                    DIRK
        You got a new car?

                    SCOTTY J.
        Yeah. Wanna see?

                    DIRK
        Sure.

CAMERA FOLLOWS them outside, they pass Reed and Todd who are
standing near the BBQ pit --

                    REED
        Hey, Dirk, c'mere and meet someone.
        This is Todd, my pal from the thing --

                    DIRK
        How are 'ya?

                    TODD
        We finally meet.

                    REED
        Remember I told you about Todd?
        He works over at the Party Boys
        Strip Club --

                    DIRK
        Oh, cool, cool. You're a dancer?

                    TODD
        Yeah, I got some moves.

                    SCOTTY J.
        -- Dirk? Are you coming --?

                    DIRK
        Yeah, okay, Scotty.
                (to Todd)
        I'll see you around. We can talk later.

CAMERA continues with Dirk and Scotty J. out to the DRIVEWAY.
They check out the USED CANDY-APPLE RED TOYOTA CORROLA.

                    SCOTTY J.
        This is it.

                    DIRK
        Cool.

```
                    SCOTTY J.
          Wanna get inside?

                    DIRK
          When did you get this?

                    SCOTTY J.
          Yesterday.

                    DIRK
          It's great.  It's really great.

                    SCOTTY J.
          Yeah, you wanna take a ride, or --

                    DIRK
          Wait a minute, wait aminute,
          waitaminute....fuckin' hell...how much time left?

                    SCOTTY J.
          Six minutes...

                    DIRK
          Oh, Shit!  Let's get back inside, come on --

Dirk starts to walk away....Scotty watches him go....Suddenly:
Scotty CHARGES Dirk from behind and starts to KISS his neck.
Dirk stumbles, pushes him away and turns:

                    SCOTTY J.
          I'm sorry, Dirk. Please. I'm sorry.

                    DIRK
          ....why'd you do that?

                    SCOTTY J.
          You look at me sometimes --

                    DIRK
          -- What?

                    SCOTTY J.
          I wanna know if you like me.

                    DIRK
          ...yeah....Scotty.

                    SCOTTY J.
          Can I kiss you?

                    DIRK
          ...Scott...I don't --

                    SCOTTY J.
          -- can I please kiss your mouth?
          Please.  Please let me.
```

                    DIRK
No.

                    SCOTTY J.
I'm really sorry. I didn't mean
to grab you....I didn't --

                    DIRK
It's alright.

                    SCOTTY J.
...I'm sorry...

                    DIRK
...it's alright.

                    SCOTTY J.
Do you wanna kiss me?

                    DIRK
Scotty.

                    SCOTTY J.
No, no. Forget it. I'm sorry.
I'm really sorry, I'm just drunk.
I'm outta my head, okay?

                    DIRK
...yeah --

                    SCOTTY J.
I'm just crazy, you know? Crazy. Right?
I'm so wasted, drunk, drunk --

                    DIRK
You wanna go back inside?

                    SCOTTY J.
Do you like me car, Dirk?

                    DIRK
What...? Yeah. Yeah.

                    SCOTTY J.
I wanted to make sure you thought it
was cool or else I was gonna take it back.

                    DIRK
Oh.

PAUSE. Dirk hesitates...then turns and walks back into the house.

                    SCOTTY J.
                    (to himself)
I love you, Dirk.

                                        CUT TO:

94   INT. JACK'S HOUSE - NIGHT - MOMENTS LATER

Jack calls out to the crowd of Party People.

                              JACK
                WE GOT TWO MINUTES, PEOPLE! TWO MINUTES!

                                                          CUT TO:

95   INT. HALLWAY - THAT MOMENT   95

CAMERA follows Little Bill as he walks the hallway to a closed
bathroom door. He opens it.

OVER LITTLE BILL'S SHOULDER, INSIDE THE BATHROOM
Little Bill's WIFE is getting FUCKED DOGGY STYLE by yet ANOTHER
YOUNG STUD. She looks at him.

                        LITTLE BILL'S WIFE
                You should be taking notes, Little Bill.

                        ANOTHER YOUNG STUD
                This is a fresh cunt, pal.

Little Bill stands a moment, then closes the door. CAMERA LEADS
him as he walks back through the party...outside to the pool
area and into the driveway for his Station Wagon.

He takes the keys from his pocket, unlocks the passenger side door,
reaches into the glove compartment and takes out a .38 REVOLVER and
AMMUNITION.

CAMERA FOLLOWS him now as he heads back across the driveway,
back through the pool area, loading the gun as he walks...

People begin counting off to the New Year --

                        PARTY PEOPLE
                10....9....8....7....

Little Bill walks into the house, down the hallway --

                        PARTY PEOPLE
                ....6....5....4....3...2...1....

Little Bill arrives at the Bathroom door and SMASHES IT OPEN:
His Wife and the Young Stud are still fucking....

                        PARTY PEOPLE (OC)
                ....HAPPY NEW YEAR!

Little Bill FIRES THE REVOLVER INTO HIS WIFE'S NAKED STOMACH.
He FIRES THE GUN AGAIN, STRIKING THE YOUNG STUD IN THE HEART.

THEY BOTH COLLAPSE AND FALL TO THE FLOOR OF THE BATHROOM.
BLOOD SPLATTERS LITTLE BILL....

...EVERYONE IN THE PARTY JUMPS AT THE SOUND OF THE GUNSHOTS...

..LITTLE BILL FIRES ANOTHER SHOT INTO HIS WIFE...

...BLOOD AND SMOKE FILL THE BATHROOM...

...LITTLE BILL TURNS AROUND, FACES THE PARTY PEOPLE AND SHOVES
THE REVOLVER IN HIS MOUTH AND PULLS THE TRIGGER...

BLOOD AND BRAINS SHOOT OUT THE BACK OF HIS SKULL AND HE COLLAPSES,
FALLING OUT OF FRAME.

TITLE CARD READS:

                         "80s"

                                                    FADE OUT.

OVER BLACK, WE HEAR THE VOICE:

                         AMBER (OC)
                    ...what about your character,
                    "Brock Landers," and what some people
                    might consider violent attitudes towards women?

                                                    CUT TO:

Sequence "C"

96   INT. DIRK'S HOUSE/BALCONY - DAY - DOCUMENTARY FOOTAGE. (16mm)   96

Dirk is doing an interview. He's unshaven, thin and sweating, wearing
sunglasses. He speaks quickly to Amber OC. (1982)

                         DIRK
                    violence...? No, what? I mean, if there's
                    something in this series of movies that's
                    like action or violence or whatever -- that's
                    the movie. Y'know? Look: I'm not saying that
                    these movies are for the whole family, but they've
                    gotalotta action and sometimes the characters
                    are women who are -- say -- spies or drug
                    smugglers or working for some organization
                    that my character is trying to....defeat.
                    We've made twenty of these films in the past
                    um...um...five years, since 77...and this kind
                    of talk has only come up in the past year
                    or so...I mean: What's the problem? So -- y'know.

                                                    CUT TO:

97   <u>INT. BROCK LANDERS BEDROOM SET - NIGHT - 16mm FILM CLIP</u>   97

    Dirk is in his underwear, asleep in bed. An actress named KC SUNSHINE
    plays in the scene with him as an Indian woman, wrapped in a sheet.
    She enters, holding a knife, coming towards Dirk...

                      AMBER (VO)
            If Brock Landers is slick with a gun he does
            so only in the vein of good and right.
            Brock protects the values of the American ideal
            and fights for causes that instill pride
            in a society where morals are hard to come by --

    Dirk wakes in the scene, struggles with KC Sunshine, knocks
    the knife from her hand and pins her down. The scene plays;

                      DIRK
        WHO SENT YOU?

                    KC SUNSHINE
        GET THE FUCK OFF ME, ASSHOLE.

                      DIRK
        LAY STILL, I'LL PUNCH YOU IN THE GOD DAMN FACE.

                    KC SUNSHINE
        FUCK OFF.

    Dirk SMACKS her then starts to KISS her breats softly.

                                  CUT TO:

98   <u>EXT. ALLEY WAY - NIGHT - 16mm FILM CLIP</u>   98 *

    In the scene, Dirk has Becky (playing a PROSTITUTE) up against
    a wall. He's right in her face, holding his fist up....The scene:

                      DIRK
            I'm onna ask once more and
            I'm onna ask you nice....WHERE THE
            FUCK IS RINGO, YOU BITCH?

                    BECKY
        Fuck you.

    Dirk SLAPS her across the face.

                    BECKY
        Ohhh...do it again, maybe I'll
        get my pussy wet next time.

    BUCK arrives playing a PIMP and aims a REVLOVER at Dirk.

                    BUCK
        HEY CRACKER-JACK, WATCHYOU DOIN' WIT MY WOMAN?

    Just then: REED appears with a GUN aimed at Buck.

                              REED
                Make another move, motherfucker
                and give me a good god damn reason
                to blow you away!

                                                    CUT TO:

99   OMITTED   99

100   OMITTED   100

101   OMITTED   101

102   OMITTED ** Director's Note: Rollergirl's Interview/TBA   102

103   OMITTED ** Director's Note: Jessie's Interview/TBA   103

104   OMITTED   104

105   INT. JACK'S HOUSE/EDITING ROOM - DAY - DOCU FOOTAGE.   105

      Jack and Dirk are sitting behind a Moviola for the
      interview with Amber. Dirk speaks very quickly...

                              DIRK
                BLOCK....uh...and idea or a movement.
                Jack will put the final touches on what
                the camera needs for editing -- but, uh --
                He allows me to block my own sex scenes.
                ...and...he gives me flexibility to work
                with the character and develop, y'know....
                I don't know of any other director's
                that would let an actor - uh - do that.

                              JACK
                I don't let you block your own sex scenes.

      Jack and Amber laugh. Dirk laughs a little less.

                                                    CUT TO:

106   EXT. VENTURA BLVD. - DUSK - DOCU. FOOTAGE.   106

      Footage of Dirk walking along the street as the sun goes down.
      Amber narrates.

                              AMBER (OC)
                For Dirk Diggler, the future is something
                to look forward to, not to fear....he is
                a creative man of many interests...film,
                poetry, karate, music and dance...he is a man
                of passion and mystery...He Is A Man. Of Lust.

                                            FADE OUT, CUT TO:

End Sequence "C"

INT. JACK'S HOUSE/EDITING ROOM - NIGHT (May 82)

Dirk and Amber, sitting in front of the Steenbeck. She flips it
off and looks to him;

                         AMBER
               It's my poem to you.

                         DIRK
               It's great. It's so great, Amber.
               You're a director now. Shit.
               Have you showed Jack?

                         AMBER
               Just you. I wanted to show you first.

                         DIRK
               It's so fuckin' good. Really.
                         (beat)
               Maybe you might want to think about
               cutting that part when Jack says that
               thing about -- y'know --

                         AMBER
               Blocking the sex --

                         DIRK
               -- yeah.

                                             CUT TO:

108 INT. JACK'S HOUSE - NIGHT - MOMENTS LATER   108

Dirk and Amber walk out and into the living room, CAMERA SWINGS
180 OVER TO: Jack and Reed, sitting at the kitchen counter;

                         JACK
               How was it?

At that moment the PHONE RINGS, CAMERA WHIPS OVER to the phone.
It rings again. Jack picks it up. DOLLY/ZOOM IN QUICK.

                         JACK
               Hello? Colonel? Wait, wait, wait.
               Yes. Calm down. Calm down. Okay.
               Right Now -- Yes -- Right Now.

He slams the phone down.

                                             CUT TO:

The Colonel is sitting in handcuffs, crying his eyes out.
Jack sits across from him, speaking through the glass.

> COLONEL
> ...she was fifteen...fifteen...I didn't
> know...Jack, you gotta believe me.

> JACK
> I believe you.

> COLONEL
> I told her not to do so much coke, but she
> wouldn't listen, she just kept doing it and
> doing it like she was a vacuum. Like she had
> a vacuum in her nose or something....
> ....next thing I know...she's got blood
> coming from her nose and...jesus...her, jesus --

> JACK
> What?

> COLONEL
> It was coming out her ass, Jack.

> JACK
> Okay. It's gonna be okay. Just relax.
> The bail is a hundred thousand dollars.
> I don't have that kind of cash --

> COLONEL
> -- I don't have any money left.

> JACK
> What do you mean? Nothing?

The Colonel shakes his head a little, doesn't answer.

> JACK
> Well...what...how?

> COLONEL
> I spent it....I spent it.

> JACK
> The films....or...I mean?

> COLONEL
> I spent it, alright? This shit gets
> expensive. Between you shooting film,
> the coke, the limos, the houses.
> It goes, alright? I spent it.

> JACK
> Alright, okay. Don't worry.

                    COLONEL
          I can't have this happen to me.
          I'm a good man, right?

                    JACK
          Yes you are.

                    COLONEL
          I didn't know -- I didn't know she was
          gonna die right there with me or I wouldn't
          have picked her up.

                    JACK
          Right. You know; you've done nothing wrong.
          I mean, look; You were just there, right?
          You didn't...I mean...you didn't do anything.

                    COLONEL
          They found something in my house, Jack.

                    JACK
          What?

                    COLONEL
          ...something...

                    JACK
          ...what are you saying? What did they find?

                    COLONEL
          ...it's my fuckin' weakness, Jack.
          They're....so small and cute I can't help
          myself, Jack. I can't help it when they're so
          small and cute, I just want to watch, I don't do
          anything, Jack. I've never touched one of them....

                    JACK
          Jesus Christ, Colonel.

                    COLONEL
          You look at me like I'm an asshole, now.

                    JACK
          ....I.....I don't....?

                    COLONEL
          I'm going to jail for a long time.

                    JACK
          -- it's okay, Colonel. It's gonna be
          fine in the end....I promise....

                    COLONEL
          Are you promising me?

     Jack doesn't answer.

                              COLONEL
                Take it back, Jack. Don't promise me anything.
                You can't help me. I'm done. I'm going to jail.
                I've done wrong and I'm going to jail for
                a long, long time.

They hold a look for a moment. A few OFFICERS come and start
to escort the Colonel away. He leans in, speaks sotto;

                              COLONEL
                Listen to me, Jack: And I'm gonna tell
                you this for you. Am I your friend?

                              JACK
                What?

                              COLONEL
                Answer me, am I your friend?

                              JACK
                Yes.

                              COLONEL
                So remember that I'm your friend and
                listen to what I tell you now: Give in, Jack.
                You've gotta give. For you, for your bussiness
                and your livelihood -- accept the future.
                Don't fight it, because you can't win.
                Look for the new blood, go to Floyd Gondolli,
                go to video, give up your battle -- the
                filmmaking is over, Jack.

The Officers take him away. Jack watches him leave. DOLLY IN CLOSE
ON JACK.

                                                   CUT TO:

110   INT. JACK'S HOUSE/OFFICE - DAY   110

CAMERA HOLDS A LOW ANGLE, LOOKING UP AT JACK, KURT and ROCKY.
They look into CAMERA. HOLD.

                              JACK
                Well there we go.

                              KURT LONGJOHN
                Yeah.

                              ROCKY
                Lot of stuff on there to learn.

                              JACK
                That's it.

                              KURT LONGJOHN
                No turning back now.

                         JACK
          The future.

                         KURT LONGJOHN
          That's right.

                         ROCKY
          The quality is, uh --

                         JACK
          It's not what we're used to.

                         KURT LONGJOHN
          We can make it work, I think.

                         ROCKY
          It's....potential...

                         KURT LONGJOHN
          Yes.

                         JACK
          You can't beat the price.

                         KURT LONGJOHN
          No you can't.

                         JACK
          This is the future and we can't deny
          it anymore because the past is too expensive.

                         KURT LONGJOHN
          I'm scared.

                         ROCKY
          Me too.

                         JACK
          It's gonna make us rich.

                         KURT LONGJOHN
          Yep.

                         ROCKY
          It's a rather pretty thing, isn't it?

REVERSE ANGLE: A new VIDEO CAMERA is sitting on the table in front of
them. This is the thing they've been discussing.

                         KURT LONGJOHN
          We can still tell good stories, Jack.

                         JACK
          No. It's about jacking off now, Kurt.
          No more stories....that's over.

                                             CUT TO:

111   <u>INT. HOT TRAXX NIGHTCLUB - NIGHT</u> (Dec.82)   111

BECKY looks into CAMERA;

                      BECKY
        I do.

JEROME looks into CAMERA;

                      JEROME
        I do too.

CU - BLACK AND WHITE SNAPSHOT
Becky and Jerome kissing. Jack as Best Man. Amber as Brides Maid.

CAMERA on the dance floor; Becky, dressed in a WHITE BRIDAL DRESS and
Jerome, dressed in a TUXEDO. Reed is dancing with them.

                      BECKY
        They made Jerome regional manager
        of the new "Pep Boys," they're building
        in Bakersfield. We're gonna move there.
        Buy a house.

                      REED
        That's great, guys. That's so great.

                      JEROME
        It's gonna be a great opportunity to run
        the store my way. Y'know. Get those guys
        off my back and run the store <u>my way</u>.

CAMERA picks up and follows Dirk who walks over to Jack's table --   *

                                              *

*

                    ANGLE, JACK'S TABLE.
                    Jack is sitting with a handsome young kid, JOHNNY DOE (aged 18.)
                    Dirk arrives;

                                        JACK
                              ...and it's tough is what I'm saying.

                                        JOHNNY DOE
                              Right.

                                        JACK
                              Hey, Dirk -- here you are. You havin'
                              a good time?

                                        DIRK
                              uh-huh.
                                        (re: Johnny Doe)
                              Who's this?

                                        JOHNNY DOE
                              Hi....I'm Johnny Doe. You're Dirk
                              Diggler -- it's great to meet you.

                                        JACK
                              Dirk, meet Johnny Doe....New Kid On The
                              Block. He's interested in the business.

                    Dirk nods his head, picks up his sunglasses from the table and
                    walks off across the dance floor. Jack turns back to Johnny Doe;

                              JACK
                    He's pretty tired, Johnny. He's also shy.
                    Anyway: What I'm saying to you is this:
                    It costs money, you got ten, fifteen people
                    standing around, and that's just to make
                    sure the lighting is right --   *

Jack continues chatting with Johnny Doe, he looks away for a moment.

JACK'S POV: Dirk meets up with Todd Parker and they walk out
the door.(40fps)

Jack turns back to Johnny Doe. Continue a bit with party stuff/etc.
Jack has his dance w/Becky.

                                                   CUT TO:

112   EXT. JACK'S POOL AREA - DAY (Jan.83)   112

     CAMERA begins with Kurt and Rocky standing nearby the VIDEO CAMERA.
     Reed is watching them try and figure it out.

     Jack is waiting patiently, working on a crossword puzzle.
     Johnny Doe is swimming in the pool.

     Rollergirl moves past and CAMERA follows her into --

                                                   CUT TO:

INT. JACK'S HOUSE - DAY - THAT MOMENT   113

     Dirk is dressed in Speedos and a headband for the scene and laying out
     some coke on the table. Rollergirl arrives, she does some --
     The television in the b.g., is tuned to MTV which is playing
     "Video Killed The Radio Star."

                          ROLLERGIRL
                    This stuff burns.

                          DIRK
                    It's crystal.

                          ROLLERGIRL
                    That's why. Shit, why didn't you
                    tell me -- you don't need to do that much --
                    You only have to do bumps with crystal.

                          DIRK
                    Yeah, well...mind your own business
                    or get your own or whatever --

                          ROLLERGIRL
                    You don't have to be mean about it --

     Rollergirl skates off. Dirk looks out the window, sees Johnny Doe
     swimming. Amber is speaking to him. CAMERA DOLLIES IN A LITTLE
     (30fps) ON DIRK.

                                                            CUT TO:

114   INT. BEDROOM - THAT MOMENT   114

     Maurice is sitting on the edge of the bed, shaking and sweating.
     Rollergirl enters and moves to a closet.

                          MAURICE
                    Hey...Rollergirl...hey.

                          ROLLERGIRL
                    What's wrong?

                          MAURICE
                    Where?

                          ROLLERGIRL
                    With you?

                          MAURICE
                    Me?-Nothing-Why?

                          ROLLERGIRL
                    You look like a wreck.

                          MAURICE
                    Shit no, I'm cool as a cucumber.

Rollergirl takes off her clothes and gets into her BIKINI.

                    ROLLERGIRL
          It's your big day -- bein' in a movie.

                    MAURICE
          Yeah.

                    ROLLERGIRL
          What you always wanted.

                    MAURICE
          I'm very thankful to Jack for
          giving me the chance.

BEAT.

                    MAURICE
          Rollergirl?

                    ROLLERGIRL
          What?

                    MAURICE
          My dick is really small.

                    ROLLERGIRL
          What?

                    MAURICE
          My dick...it's small.

                    ROLLERGIRL
          How small?

                    MAURICE
          Really small.

                    ROLLERGIRL
          Well...uh...so?

                    MAURICE
          So I can't do this.

                    ROLLERGIRL
          Can you get a boner?

                    MAURICE
          I don't think so.

                    ROLLERGIRL
          Well...

                    MAURICE
          Please. Can you help me?

                    ROLLERGIRL
How?

                    MAURICE
I dunno.

                    ROLLERGIRL
If you've got a small dick,
there's really nothing I can do, Maurice.

                    MAURICE
....right....right....

                    ROLLERGIRL
Just go for it, man.

                    MAURICE
What do you mean?

                    ROLLERGIRL
Just go for it...who cares if you've got
a small dick. It's how you use it, right?
You can get a boner, I bet. I know you can.

                    MAURICE
I guess.

                    ROLLERGIRL
Be a man about it.

                    MAURICE
Right. Right. I have to be a man about it.
I have to do this...I have to show my brothers
in Puerto Rico the lifestyle that I'm living.
I can do it...I can do it.

                    ROLLERGIRL
You'll do fine.

                    MAURICE
Right.

                    ROLLERGIRL
C'mon.

                    MAURICE
No...no...I wanna stay here for a bit --

                    ROLLERGIRL
Okay....I'll be out there.

She exits. HOLD with Maurice a moment.

                                        CUT TO:

115 OMITTED   115

116   INT. BATHROOM - DAY - THAT MOMENT   116

Dirk enters, closes the door, looks in the mirror;

                         DIRK
              ...yeah,yeah,yeah...You look good, ready.

Dirk does some quick KARATE moves, then turns his BACK TO THE CAMERA.
He unzips his pants, looks down at his cock. His body starts to move
a little, slowly at first then faster as he tries to masturbate.

                         DIRK
              C'mon...c'mon...c'mon....I'm a star.
              I'm a star, I'm a rock and roll star.
              And My Cock Can Get Hard.
              C'mon...c'mon...c'mon....I'm a star.
              I'm a star, I'm a star, I'm a star.

The DOOR to the Bathroom is SUDDENLY OPENED by Scotty J. who catches
Dirk in the mirror with his pants down, speaking to himself;

                         DIRK
              --what the fuck--

Scotty exits quickly. Dirk pulls up his pants and exits --

                                                          CUT TO:

117   EXT. JACK'S HOUSE/POOL AREA - DAY - MOMENTS LATER   117

Jack is still sitting in the same spot. Johnny Doe is drying off.
Dirk comes charging out --

                         DIRK
              I'm ready to shoot.

                         JACK
              We need twenty minutes.

                         DIRK
              No. I'm ready now. It's gotta be now.

                         JACK
              Twenty minutes.

                         DIRK
              Fuck it. Hey, No, Hey. Jack.
              I'm ready now...my cock is ready now.
              I'm ready to fuck...let's go now.

                         JACK
              Yeah, well...NO. Get me? You wanna
              start something here, Dirk?

                    DIRK
          I wanna start fucking...who is it gonna be?

                    JACK
          What?

                    DIRK
          Who do you want to fuck, me or him?

.Dirk points at Johnny Doe.

                    JOHNNY DOE
          Me...what?

                    DIRK
          Shut up.

                    JOHNNY DOE
          I didn't do anything to you.

                    DIRK
          You're not an actor, man. You got no
          bussiness being here -- you're not an actor --

                    JOHNNY DOE
          Yes I am.

                    DIRK
          No: I'm an actor, man. I'm a real actor.

                    JOHNNY DOE
          Shut-up.

Dirk MAKES A QUICK KARATE-TYPE MOVE TOWARDS JOHNNY DOE, WHO FLINCHES,
BUT QUICKLY GETS INTO A KARATE-STANCE OF HIS OWN.

                    JOHNNY DOE
          HEY, MAN, DON'T.

                    DIRK
          SHUT-UP. SHUT-UP.

                    JACK
          Dirk, you need to settle down.
          Go inside, have a drink and
          mellow this off...you understand?

                    DIRK
          I'm ready to shoot.

                    JACK
          Well I'm not.

                    DIRK
          I'm not gonna tell you again, Jack:

                    JACK
-- Get outta here.

                    DIRK
...What...?

                    JACK
Get off my set, get outta my house.

                    DIRK
...you...what?

                    JACK
Leave.

                    DIRK
No.

                    JACK
You don't want to do this --
the state you're in, Dirk.

                    DIRK
Whatta you mean, state? State?
State of California? Yeah, I'm in
the state of California.

                    JACK
Jesus Christ.

                    DIRK
What are you, Jack, Jack, hey --

                    JACK
You're high and you need to sleep it off.
You've been up for two days.

                    DIRK
I haven't been up for two days.

                    JACK
Whatever. You're high and you need
to come down. Sleep it off, Dirk.

                    DIRK
YOU DON'T TELL ME ANYTHING.

                    JACK
Get the fuck outta here.

                    DIRK
YOU'RE NOT THE BOSS OF ME.

                    JACK
Yes I am.

                    DIRK
          ARE YOU THE KING? HUH?

                    JACK
          Jesus Christ. MOVE. GET OUT. GO.

Jack starts to prod Dirk a little with a slight PUSH.

                    DIRK
          DON'T YOU FUCKIN TOUCH ME, MAN.

Jack SLAPS Dirk across the face. HOLD. Dirk is shocked.
Everyone has stopped what they're doing by now and is watching
nervously. Amber comes over.

                    AMBER
          Dirk, honey, why don't we go for a walk--

                    DIRK
          YOU SHUT UP, TOO. YOU'RE NOT THE MOTHER
          OF ME OR MY BOSS. YOU'RE NOT MY MOTHER.

                    AMBER
          Dirk, please, honey.

                    JACK
          Reed --

Reed comes over to the fight.

                    JACK
          Take him home, Reed. I don't need this.

                    DIRK
          No. No. I wanna shoot the scene.
          I'm ready to shoot the scene. I'm fine.

                    JACK
          I don't want you here.

                    DIRK
          Look...it's over...alright.
          I'm done...now I'm ready to shoot.
          I'm calm, my cock is cool and ready.

                    REED
          Why don't we go home, Dirk?

                    DIRK
          I'm the one with the cock, I'm the
          one with the big fucking cock, so let's go --

                    JACK
          You listen to me now, kid --

                    DIRK
          DON'T CALL ME A KID. I'LL FUCK YOU UP.
          YOU WANNA SEE ME KICK SOME ASS. YOU WANNA
          FUCK WITH ME, I KNOW KARATE. SO C'MON.

                    REED
          Dirk, let's be cool, let's --

                    DIRK
          I'm the biggest star here -- THAT'S
          THE WAY IT IS: I WANNA FUCK. AND
          IT'S MY BIG DICK, SO EVERYBODY GET READY.

                    JACK
          Not anymore.

                    DIRK
          WHAT? What "not anymore?"

                    JACK
          Your dick.

                    DIRK
          WHAT, WHAT? SAY IT.

                    JACK
          I've seen you push thirteen inches, you'd be
          lucky if you could manage six today -- all the
          coke you got in you. You're not ready to fuck,
          your dick's not getting hard today, kid.

                    DIRK
          DON'T YOU TALK ABOUT ME LIKE THAT, JACK.

                    JACK
          Alright: You're fired. Okay?
          You understand? You're fired.
          Get outta here now. NOW.

                    DIRK
          WHAT? WHAT IS THAT? WHAT IS THAT?

                    JACK
          Just leave, Dirk. Leave RIGHT NOW.

                    DIRK
          My cock is READY. YOU WANNA SEE?
          HUH? YOU WANNA SEE MY BIG FUCKIN' COCK?

Suddenly, blood begins to pour violently from his nose. He cups
his hand over his nose, hides his embarrassment;

                    DIRK
          FUCK THIS, FUCK THIS, FUCK YOU.
          FUCK ALL OF YOU. YOU'RE NOT MY BOSSES.
          NO ONE IS THE KING OF ME.

Dirk runs away gets behind the wheel of his Corvette and tears off
bleeding all the way --

Reed, Jack, Scotty, Amber, Johnny Doe and the rest of the crew
watch him go.

                                                        FADE OUT.

118   OMITTED
                                                        CUT TO:

119   INT. RECORDING STUDIO - DAY (Mar. 83)   Sequence "D"

Dirk stands in front of a microphone wearing head phones.
The ENGINEER in the booth speaks;

                        ENGINEER
            Okay...Dirk you ready?

                        DIRK
            I was born ready, man.

                        ENGINEER
            Okay...Dirk Diggler Demo Tape,
            "You Got The Touch," Take seven....

The BAND kicks in and Dirk begins to sing his song. It's a cross
between Kenny Loggins/Survivor and any "Rocky" anthem.

                        DIRK
            YOU GOT THE TOUCH...YOU GOT THE POWER.
            YEEEEAAAHHHH. AFTER ALL IS SAID AND DONE,
            YOU NEVER WALK, YOU NEVER RUN, YOU'RE A WINNER.

                                                        CUT TO:

120   INT. RECORDING BOOTH - LATER

Dirk, Reed and the Engineer are mixing. The song PLAYS.

                        DIRK
            Is the bass taking away from the vocals?

                        ENGINEER
            Well...a little...but not really too much.

                        DIRK
            Let's take down the bass and let's take
            up the vocals.

                                                        CUT TO:

121   INT. RECORDING STUDIO - LATER   121

        Dirk is singing. Reed is playing guitar on a BALLAD called,
        "FEEL THE HEAT." CAMERA DOLLIES IN ON THEM.

                              DIRK
                    THE HEAT WILL ROCK YOU, THE HEAT WILL ROLL YOU
                    BABY DON'T YOU KNOW
                    MY HEAT WILL MOVE YOU IN YOUR SOUL
                    C'MON, C'MON, C'MON
                    LOVE ME TODAY, LOVE ME TOMORROW
                    ALL DAY, ALL NIGHT, YOU FEEL MY BEAT

                           REED/DIRK
                    FEEL, FEEL, FEEL....MY HEAT.

                                                            CUT TO:

122   INT. RECORDING BOOTH - CONTINUED   122

        Dirk, Reed and the Engineer. Scotty and Todd are sitting around.
        making phone calls, eating the free food, etc.

                            ENGINEER
                    So...what do you think?

                              DIRK
                    Well I think that...maybe we could
                    speed it up a little -- it's --

                            ENGINEER
                    It's a ballad. I thought that --

                              DIRK
                    We'll just speed it up a couple octaves.
                    ...cause that might make it cooler,
                    people like it when slow songs...y'know...
                    when they're a little fast....it's cooler.

                                                            CUT TO:

123   INT. JACK'S LIVING ROOM - DAY   123

        Jack is directing a scene with an AMATEUR PORN ACTRESS and JOHNNY DOE.
        They're on the couch in Jack's living room. Johnny Doe has adopted
        more of a celebrity attitude.

                            AMATEUR
                    Is he gonna fuck me in the ass?

                              JACK
                    Is that what you want?

                            AMATEUR
                    It would be nice.

                              JACK
                    Johnny: Fuck her in the ass.

                            JOHNNY DOE
                    Lock and Load, Jack.

          He takes a seat behind the VIDEO CAMERA and says;

                              JACK
                    Alright, friends; let's get it over with.

                                             DISSOLVE TO:

124   EXT. BAKERSFIELD HOUSE - NIGHT   124

          Establishing shot of a small little house with a white picket fence.
          From the house we hear the sounds of SCREAMING AND VIOLENCE.

                                             CUT TO:

125   INT. BAKERSFIELD HOUSE - NIGHT - THAT MOMENT   125

          Becky is crouched in the corner of the kitchen. Jerome is standing
          above her, dressed in his Pep Boys uniform.

                            JEROME
                    YOU FUCKIN' WHORE, YOU'RE A FUCKIN' WHORE.

                            BECKY
                    Please, Jerome, don't --

                            JEROME
                    You probably liked those big cocks, huh?

                            BECKY
                    Don't --

                            JEROME
                    I'll tell you about a big cock -- yeah,
                    you want my cock to be bigger, don't you?

                            BECKY
                    No, baby, please, please --

          Jerome SMACKS Becky in the face --

                                             DISSOLVE TO:

126   INT. VALLEY BANK - DAY   126

          Buck is dressed like a regular joe in a suit, holding a briefcase
          on his lap, sitting patiently. Jessie St. Vincent is sitting with
          him, holding his hand. He's approached by a middle aged white male
          BANK WORKER. CAMERA DOLLIES IN.

                            BANK WORKER
                    Mr. Swope?

                         BUCK
          Yeah, that's me. Hello.

                         BANK WORKER
          You have a copy of your loan application?

                         BUCK
          Yes I do.

                         BANK WORKER
          Good. You wanna follow me?

                                             CUT TO:

127   INT. JACK'S HOUSE/AMBER'S BEDROOM - DAY   127 *

      CAMERA DOLLIES IN ON Rollergirl and Amber. They're playing
      backgammon and talking on Amber's bed, doing coke and smoking cigs.

                         AMBER
          I was gonna take a pottery class at
          Everywoman's Village --

                         ROLLERGIRL
          Oh, oh. I wanna do that.

                         AMBER
          We'll do it, then. It's Monday,
          Wednesday, Friday at three.

                         ROLLERGIRL
          Do you think I should -- I was thinking something?

                         AMBER
          What?

                         ROLLERGIRL
          I was gonna see about taking the GED.
          Do you know what that is?

                         AMBER
          For High School, to graduate?

                         ROLLERGIRL
          Yeah. It's like -- so I can get my
          diploma -- 'cause I feel bad that I
          never did it. I think you were right.
          I think you right --

                         AMBER
          You should do it. That would be great
          for you -- you know -- cause if you
          wanted, Rollergirl, you could do anything.

Amber turns her head to something OC. AMBER'S POV: Jack is directing another scene in the living room between TWO YOUNG PORN ACTRESSES with fake breasts who we have never seen before.

Amber motions to Rollergirl, who gets up and SLAMS THE DOOR.

                                                              CUT TO:

128/128A INT. DIRK'S HOUSE - DAY   (2x)   128/128A *

Dirk, Reed and Scotty J. are sitting around. Todd enters holding an envelope. DOLLY IN SUPER-QUICK.

                         TODD
              I'm back.

                         DIRK
              Perfect timing.

They move to a table and anxiously set out some coke.

                                                              CUT TO:

129   INT. HOT TRAXX NIGHTCLUB - DAY   129 *

CAMERA DOLLIES IN ON MAURICE. The club is closed and empty.
Maurice sits at the bar, writing a letter. An envelope and a
videotape are placed nearby. Following is SUB-TITLED;

                    MAURICE (VO)
              Dear brothers: Here's an example
              of me with women in Los Angeles.
              I sleep with women here all the time...

                                                              CUT TO:

130   INT. APARTMENT BLDG./PUERTO RICO - DAY   130

Maurice's two BROTHERS rip open the envelope, read the letter
and slip the tape into their VCR that's wired to a crappy black
and white television. CAMERA DOLLIES IN ON THE BROTHERS.

                    BROTHER #1
                (in Spanish, sub-titled)
              Oh my God --

                    BROTHER #2
                (in Spanish, sub-titled)
              -- it's so...so...it looks like a peanut.

                                                              CUT TO:

131   <u>INT. VALLEY BANK - DAY - CONTINUED</u>   131

        CAMERA DOLLIES IN ON BUCK. He's speaking to the BANK WORKER.

                      BUCK
             That's what Buck's Super Stereo World
             is all about -- the customer. People wanna
             know what they're getting into technically
             and I have the specific technical hi-fi
             background to answer any technical question
             that someone might have -- I've been into
             sound equipment for long enough to know what
             a guy wants when he walks right in the door --
             and that's the personel touch that Buck's Super
             Stereo World is gonna have --

                                  CUT TO:

132   <u>INT. JACK'S HOUSE/AMBER'S ROOM - DAY - CONTINUED</u>

    Amber and Rollergirl are sitting in front of a pile of coke that's
laid out on top of a big book....

                     AMBER
             I miss my two sons -- my little Andrew
             and my Dirk -- I miss them both so much.
             I always felt like Dirk was my baby, my new baby.
             Don't you miss, Dirk?

                  ROLLERGIRL
        Yeah.

                     AMBER
             He's so fucking talented. The bastard.
             I love him, Rollergirl, I mean; I really
             love the little jerk.

                  ROLLERGIRL
             I love you, Mom. I want you to to be
             my mother, Amber. Are you my Mom?
             I'll ask you if you're my mother and
             you say, "yes." OK? -- Are you my mother -- ?

                    AMBER
        Yes, honey. Yes.

    They cry and hug and laugh and do more coke, smoke more cigs, etc.

                                    CUT TO:

INT. RECORDING STUDIO - DAY

> CAMERA DOLLIES IN QUICK. Dirk and Reed are violently haggling
> in an office of the Recording Studio with the MANAGER.

                          DIRK
            C'mon, man, c'mon, c'mon, alright --

                          MANAGER
            I can't let you take the tapes until
            the bill is paid in full.

                          DIRK
            That makes a lot of sense.

                          REED
            Wait, wait, wait. How can he pay
            the price of the demo if he can't
            take the demo tapes to a record company?

                          MANAGER
            That's not my problem. My job is to
            collect payment before we hand over the tapes.

                          REED
            You can't get a record contract if
            the record company can't hear what you've got.

                          DIRK
            OK: Wait a minute - have you heard my tape?
            Huh? Have you even heard it? I'm gauranteed
            to get a record deal because my stuff is so good.
            Once that happens, I'll pay you --

                          MANAGER
            It's not gonna happen. This is a Catch-22,
            I understand. You're saying this thing
            and I get it but I just won't let it happen.

                          DIRK
            A catch-what?

                                            CUT TO:

134 INT. JACK'S HOUSE/AMBER'S ROOM - NIGHT - CONTINUED   134

Amber and Rollergirl, pacing around the room, talking, crying, etc.

                          AMBER
            I don't wanna do this anymore, honey.
            I can't. I just can't.
                          ROLLERGIRL
            What?

                          AMBER
          Have fun now, let's keep going and going
          and going tonight -- because it's over.
          There's too many things --

                          ROLLERGIRL
          Okay. Okay.

                          AMBER
          Let's go walk.

                          ROLLERGIRL
          I don't wanna leave the room.

                          AMBER
          Me either. OHHHHHHHHH. I love you, honey.

                          ROLLERGIRL
          I love you, Mom.

     They laugh and laugh and laugh and smoke, talk, walk.

                                           DISSOLVE TO:

135   INT. VALLEY BANK - DAY - CONTINUED   135

     Buck and Jessie across the desk from the Bank Worker, who looks up
     from the file and says;

                          BANK WORKER
          Mr. Swope.....we can't help you.

                          BUCK
          ...I have all the papers, all the
          things in order, yes? I mean, it's all --

                          BANK WORKER
          Yes. But we can't give you a loan. I'm sorry.

                          BUCK
          ....why...?

                          BANK WORKER
          .....Mr. Swope: You're a pornographer.
          And this bank is not in bussiness to
          support pornography --

                          BUCK
          I'm not a pornographer, I'm an actor.

                          BANK WORKER
          I'm sorry.

                                    BUCK
                No, no, no, please. This is...this is
                a new bussiness for me, a real thing
                that I want to do and a real thing that
                I can do, please, I mean -- this is not a joke --

                                    BANK WORKER
                I'm sorry.

                                    BUCK
                Please, now, please, just wait one minute
                here -- because there's gotta be some way --

                                    BANK WORKER
                ...I'm sorry...

                                    BUCK
                Well this is not fair --

                                    BANK WORKER
                This financial institution can't endorse
                pornography, you've got to understand --

                                    BUCK
                I'm an actor.

                                    BANK WORKER
                Please. Now I'm sorry.

                                                        DISSOLVE TO:

136   INT. HORNER PRODUCTIONS - VAN NUYS - DAY   136

        CAMERA (STEADICAM) follows Jack around his new OFFICES. Posters
        of his films with Johnny Doe, Amber, Rollergirl, Buck and some
        other's we've never seen cover the walls.

        A WAREHOUSE area is shipping out boxes of VHS VIDEOCASSETTE'S.
        CAMERA breezes past an EDITING ROOM where Kurt Longjohn and Rocky are
        sitting in front of two 3/4 machines, cutting a new Jack Horner film
        with Johnny Doe doing some Karate-moves reminiscent of Dirk Diggler.

        Jack continues walking into the RECEPTION AREA where TWO UNIFORMED
        POLICE OFFICERS are standing.

                                    OFFICER
                Jack Horner?

                                    JACK
                Yeah, what is it?

                                    OFFICER
                There was an accident yesterday --   *

                                                        CUT TO:

137 INT. DIRK'S HOUSE - ANOTHER DAY   137 *

   Dirk is in his bedroom. CAMERA ZOOMS/DOLLIES in SUPER QUICK
   on him doing a line of coke. Reed comes into the room, quick;

         REED
     Oh, fuck, Dirk.

         DIRK
     What?

         REED
     You know that kid Johnny Doe?

         DIRK
     No.

         REED
     Y'know, the kid from --

         DIRK
     What about him?

         REED
     He died. He got in a car accident.
     Couple nights ago...and he died.
     He like, went through the windshield
     or something. Fuckin' shit. Dead.

         DIRK
     For real?

         REED
     Yeah. He's dead. Can you believe that?

         DIRK
     That's gotta hurt, goin through a windsheild.
     It's tough luck.

   Dirk does another line of coke. The PHONE RINGS and Dirk answers.
   DOLLY/ZOOM IN QUICK.

         DIRK
     Hello? Becky? Becky-what? What?

            SPLIT SCREEN;

138 INT. BECKY'S HOUSE/BAKERSFIELD - DAY - THAT MOMENT 138

   Becky is locked in her bedroom on the phone with Dirk.
   OC outside the bedroom, we can hear Jerome YELLING and SCREAMING.

         BECKY
     I think Jerome is gonna kill me, Dirk.
     Please. Please come and help me.

                    DIRK
          Well....where are you, I don't know
          where you are --

                    BECKY
          I need you to save me, Dirk --
          if he catches me on the phone, I'm dead.

                    DIRK
          Tell me where you are.

                    BECKY
          ...okay...okay...OH SHIT. He's
          coming in -- okay -- okay -- meet
          me at Denny's in Bakersfield --
          on Colfax Blvd. Please hurry.

                    DIRK
          Okay. I'm comin' right now, right now.
          I'm comin right now to kick some ass, Becky.

SPLIT SCREEN/CAMERA stays with Becky as she hangs up the phone.
The DOOR to the BEDROOM IS SMASHED OPEN by Jerome -- he GRABS her
by the hair of her head and throws her across the room and into
the KITCHEN.

                    BECKY
          Please don't do anything to me, Jerome.
          Please. Please. I ask.

                    JEROME
          Think your Miss Fuckin Movie Star with
          a dick in your mouth? Huh? You're gonna
          tell me -- tell it to me or I'm gonna break
          your fuckin' jaw.

                    BECKY
          I don't know what you want me --

                    JEROME
          -- I want you to tell me that you liked
          getting fucked by those men in those movies.
          I want you to tell me that you loved getting
          shit in your face -- YOU FUCKIN SAY IT, CUNT.

                    BECKY
          ...I liked it...

                    JEROME
          Do you like big dicks?

                    BECKY
          I don't know what you want me to --

                    JEROME
          SAY IT.

                            BECKY
            Yes.

Jerome LEANS DOWN AND PUNCHES BECKY IN THE FACE. HOLD.
He catches his breath and walks out of the kitchen.

Becky, crouched into a corner, bleeding from her nose and mouth
reaches for a large FRYING PAN on the floor --

                                            CUT TO:

139 INT. DIRK'S HOUSE - DAY - THAT MOMENT   139 *

     Dirk grabs his keys and his jacket and heads for the door....

                            REED
            Where you goin'?

                            DIRK
            Gotta go kick some ass, man.

     He stops a moment and heads back into his bedroom....grabs his
     coke in a newspaper fold and makes a dash for the door --

                                            CUT TO:

140 EXT. DIRK'S HOUSE - DAY - THAT MOMENT   140

     Dirk exits and gets in his car QUICK. DOLLY/ZOOM IN FAST.

                                            CUT TO:

141 INT. BECKY'S HOUSE - DAY - CONTINUED   141

     CAMERA DOLLIES in front of Jerome as he walks out of the kitchen.
     In the b.g., Becky appears with the frying pan in her hand...

     She SMASHES THE FRYING PAN ACROSS THE BACK OF JEROME'S SKULL.
     He falls...she STANDS OVER HIM, STRIKING HIM AGAIN AND AGAIN.

                            BECKY
            DON'T - YOU - EVER - TOUCH - ME.

     She runs out the door --

                                            CUT TO:

142 EXT. BAKERSFIELD HOUSE - EVENING - THAT MOMENT   142

     Becky runs from the house and off down the street. HOLD.

                                            CUT TO:

INT. DIRK'S CORVETTE - MOVING - MOMENTS LATER

Dirk is driving quickly through Laurel Canyon and trying to
do a few things; 1) He's trying to light a cigarette with matches,
2) he's trying to find a cassette tape to play and 3) he's trying
to brush his hair in the rearview mirror....

CU. DIRK
the cigarette falls from his mouth and he leans down, OUT OF FRAME
to pick it up.....the car starts drifting towards a TELEPHONE POLE
that is fifteen yards ahead....Dirk gets the cigarette, comes
up INTO FRAME, looks ahead and blinks;

Dirk's Corvette SLAMS INTO THE TELEPHONE POLE.

CAMERA DOLLIES IN ON DIRK, BEHIND THE WHEEL. He shakes his head,
looks around in a daze. A PEDESTRIAN runs over;

                    PEDESTRIAN
          You alright, pal?

                    DIRK
          My fuckin' car, my car....my Corvette.

                    PEDESTRIAN
          Holy shit, you slammed right into this --

Dirk puts the car in reverse and backs away.

                    PEDESTRIAN
          I don't think you should drive the car.

                    DIRK
          Fuck you.

Dirk drives off with the front of the Corvette SHREDDING along
the pavement.

                                        CUT TO:

144   INT. BAKERSFIELD DENNY'S - NIGHT (LATER)   144

Becky is sitting at the counter. A few seats over from her is an
older man, MR. BROWN (late 60s)   He wears an old grey suit,

                    MR. BROWN
          Are you alright, ma'am?

                    BECKY
          What?

                    MR. BROWN
          Are you going to be alright?
          You seem....you've been sitting there.
          A while now. And I want to know if
          you're going to be alright.

HOLD. Becky looks down.

                    MR. BROWN
          Do you want to order something? A bowl of soup?

                    BECKY
          My friend was supposed to come
          here and get me, but he hasn't come.

                    MR. BROWN
          Yes. Well why don't you let me buy you
          some soup while you wait for your friend?

                    BECKY
          No. No. I'm not hungry.

                    Mr. BROWN
          Please. Please. I want to help you.
          This is not...this is something...you see,
          an act of kindess, I'm trying to do
          something good....to help you...for no
          other reason....other than....just to help.

Mr. Brown reaches into his pocket, takes out a quarter and
places it on the counter in front of Becky.

                    MR. BROWN
          Why don't you try calling your friend?

BEAT. Becky looks at the quarter. CAMERA HOLDS ON QUARTER.

                    MR. BROWN (OC)
          Use the quarter, young lady.

                                             CUT TO:

145   INT. DIRK'S GARAGE - NIGHT   145

          Dirk rants and raves, verging on tears, circling the car.
          Scotty, Reed and Todd are now home and looking at the damage;

                    REED
          How fast were you going?

                    DIRK
          Fuck, I dunno. Ninety.

                    SCOTTY J.
          Ninety miles an hour?

                    DIRK
          Shit, yeah. I'm lucky I'm not dead.

                    TODD
          This is a lot of damage.

                    REED
          At least it's driveable.

                    DIRK
          It's not driveable, look at it.

OC we hear the PHONE RINGING. Scotty moves to get it.

                    DIRK
          Just let it ring, we gotta deal with this --

                    REED
          At least it still works, Dirk.

                    DIRK
          You can't just drive a Corvette down
          the street looking like that, Reed.
          C'mon, man. Be reasonable.

                    REED
          How you gonna pay for it?

                    DIRK
          -- I'll find a way to pay for it.
          This is top priority, Reed:
          My car has got to get fixed.

                    TODD
          It could be like two - three thousand
          dollars worth of damage, Dirk.

                    DIRK
          So?

                    TODD
          I dunno.

                    DIRK
          We gotta get those fuckin' demo tapes, too.
          I mean it...let's go kick that guys ass
          or something...if we could get those demo
          tapes, then we get the record deal, then
          the Vette gets fixed. You cannot drive
          a Crovette down the street looking like this,
          you just can't.

                                        CUT TO:

146 INT. DENNY'S - NIGHT - MOMENTS LATER   146

     Becky is sitting in a booth across from the Mr. Brown. She's crying.

                    BECKY
          I don't know where to go. I don't
          have anywhere to go, I can't get anywhere.

                        MR. BROWN
            It's alright. It's alright, young lady.

                        BECKY
            I'm so sorry to make you hear this.

                        MR. BROWN
            I want to help you.

                        BECKY
            No, I can't.

                        MR. BROWN
            You need help. You need someplace to
            sleep and to wash. I want to help you.

                        BECKY
            You're a nice man.

    BEAT.

    End Sequence "D"   CUT TO BLACK: *

147 OMITTED   147 *

148 OMITTED   148 *

149 OMITTED   149 *

150 OMITTED   150

    TITLE CARD: "Six Months Later"
                                            CUT TO:

151 OMITTED   151 *

152 OMITTED   152 *

153 OMITTED   153 *

154 OMITTED   154 *

155   INT. HEARING ROOM - COURT BUILDING - DAY   155

Amber is sitting in a room with a long desk, a few chairs and
fluorescent lights. A middle aged female JUDGE enters and greets her;

                    JUDGE
Hello. You must be Maggie?

                    AMBER
Yes.

                    JUDGE
I'm Kathleen O'Malley. The judge.

                    AMBER
Yes.

                    JUDGE
You have a lawyer with you?

                    AMBER
No. I don't. I do not.

They sit in silence. The Judge looks over a couple of files.
Moments later, Amber's ex-husband, THOMAS (late 30s) steps in
with his LAWYER. They all take seats.

                    LAWYER
Hello, Judge.

Introductions happen, etc. BEAT. The Judge looks over some files;

                    JUDGE
You've been divorced for six years?

                    AMBER
Yes. Since 1977.

                    JUDGE
                (to lawyer)
And the agreement on the money settlement
was taken care of?

                    LAWYER
Yes.

                    JUDGE
So. What we're talking about then
is coming to an agreement on custody of Andrew.

                    AMBER
Yes.

                    JUDGE
What was decided during the divorce?

                    LAWYER
Initially. Andrew went with his father,
and visitation was given to his mother on --
                (looks at a paper)
-- from Saturday Noon to Sunday at seven.
With his mother entitled to bring Andrew
to her home or any reasonable place.

                    JUDGE
                (to Amber)
Was that the understanding?

                    AMBER
Yes.

                    JUDGE
And why wasn't that visiting privilege honored?

                    THOMAS
Well, it was for a time --

                    AMBER
I only saw him twice.

                    THOMAS
It said, "reasonable place," and I didn't
think a house of drugs and prostitution
and pornography was that.

                    JUDGE
I'm sorry, what is it that you --

                    THOMAS
My ex-wife is involved in the pornography
business -- I didn't think that environment
was a safe place for my son.

                    AMBER
          This is not right. My son was never
          exposed to pornographic material or
          drugs or any of these things, my husband
          just assumed --

                    THOMAS
          I saw it with my own eye.

PAUSE. Amber has no response. The Judge looks down at the file.

                    JUDGE
          Did you register this as a complaint?

                    LAWYER
          My client didn't officially register,
          but I think the circumstance called
          for something immediate -- for the
          safety of the child.

                    JUDGE
          How old is the boy now?

                    THOMAS
          He's twelve.

                    AMBER
          He'll be thirteen next month.

                    JUDGE
          Where do you live now?

                    THOMAS
          We live in Long Beach. I have a job
          there and my new wife is home with him.
                    (pause)
          You see, the problem is Judge, is that
          my ex-wife is a sick...she is a very sick
          person and she needs help. She deals in
          drugs and sex for a living --

                    AMBER
          I don't do drugs.

                    LAWYER
          You're honor, she has been in and out
          of trouble with the law on quite a few
          occasions regarding this sort of thing.

                    AMBER
          No. No. Not anymore.

CAMERA HOLDS ON AMBER. She watches the Judge. OC there's the
sound of papers shuffling.

                    JUDGE (OC)
          Have you ever been arrested?

                              AMBER
                   Yes.

                              JUDGE (OC)
                   When was the last time you were
                   arrested....what was the charge....?

         CAMERA DOLLIES IN CLOSE ON AMBER.

                                                        CUT TO:

156   EXT. ALLEY-WAY BEHIND THE COURT BUILDING - DAY - LATER.   156

      Amber leans against a wall, crying her eyes out. HOLD.

                                                        CUT TO:

      TITLE CARD, OVER BLACK: "Sunday, December 11, 1983"

157   INT. LIMOUSINE - NIGHT - MOVING.   157

      CAMERA'S POV is a CAMCORDER operated by KURT LONGJOHN. JACK, dressed
      in a tuxedo, sits in the back of the limo with ROLLERGIRL, who's
      wearing a full-legnth fur coat, lingere underneath.

                              JACK (into CAMERA)
                   Okay, okay, okay. Welcome to the experiment.
                   This is Jack Horner, coming to you from the
                   inside of a limousine that at this moment
                   is heading West down Ventura Blvd. I have
                   with me -- a little princess in the world
                   of adult film -- the lovely Miss Rollergirl.

                              ROLLERGIRL
                   Hello, hello, howdy.

                              JACK
                   Are you ready to do what we're gonna do?

                              ROLLERGIRL
                   Ready, ready. Ready like Freddy.

                              JACK
                   We are On The Lookout. That's what
                   we'll call this -- On The Lookout.
                   We're just gonna drive on down Ventura,
                   heading west, like I said -- and see
                   what we find. Maybe we find some new,
                   young stud who wants to take a shot
                   and get hot and heavy with Rollergirl
                   back here in the limo -- and we'll capture
                   it on video. This is a first, ladies and
                   gentleman. A first in porn history.
                   Who knows what could happen....?
                   Maybe we come across some guy, maybe some girl?
                   See if they'd like to get soft and sticky?

158   EXT. EL PUEBLO MOTEL - NIGHT   158

    Establishing shot of a crap motel in Studio City. Dirk's DAMAGED
    CORVETTE is parked out front with a U-HALL connected.

                                                          CUT TO:

159   INT. EL PUEBLO MOTEL - THAT MOMENT   159

    Dirk, Reed, Todd and Scotty J. have moved into a small motel
    with two beds and a fold-out couch. Scotty is sitting on one
    bed watching television dressed in his UNION 76 GAS STATION UNIFORM.

    Dirk is getting dressed, Reed is trying to get his attention;

                        DIRK
    Where the fuck is Todd?

                        REED
    C'mon, Dirk, seriously --

                        DIRK
    What? I dunno, okay? Okay. I don't know.

                        REED
    We have to sell your car.

                        DIRK
    I will not do it, Reed.

                        REED
    What else is there to do, Dirk?
    Huh? We have nothing left.

                        DIRK
    I worked way to fucking hard for
    that car...what am I supposed to do...?

                        REED
    It solves all our problems.

                        DIRK
    I will not sell my Corvette: Simple as that.
    Where the fuck is Todd? Where are my jeans?

                      SCOTTY
    What are you looking for?

                        DIRK
    My jeans --

                      SCOTTY
    The cool ones with the thing?

                    DIRK
          All my jeans are cool, Scotty.

                         SCOTTY
          Sorry.

Todd enters and holds up an ENVELOPE.

                         TODD
          Got it.

                         DIRK
          Where the fuck have you been?

                         TODD
          Getting some shit...

Dirk notices that Todd is wearing the JEANS he was looking for.

                         DIRK
          What the fuck is that?

                         TODD
          What?

                         DIRK
          Those are my jeans, Todd. I've
          been looking for those.

                         TODD
          You said I could borrow them.

                         DIRK
          I never said that.

                         TODD
          I thought you did.

                         SCOTTY
          Can I come with you, Dirk?

                         DIRK
          Give me my fuckin jeans back, Todd. Seriously.

                         TODD
          Sorry.

Todd gets out of his his jeans and gives them over to Dirk,
who puts them on as Reed and Scotty look on;

                         REED
          Dirk, please -- we gotta deal with
          this money situation.

                         DIRK
          Yeah, yeah, yeah.

                         SCOTTY
            Where are you goin' Dirk?

                         DIRK
              Goin' out.

                         SCOTTY J.
            Can I go with you?

       .Dirk is out the door.

                                                      CUT TO:

160   INT. LIMO - PARKED - NIGHT - CONTINUED   160

       The limo is pulled over and Jack is speaking through the window
       to some YOUNG COLLEGE STUDENT, wearing a backpack. (This kid
       is one of the boys who was making sexual gestures to Rollergirl
       earlier in the movie.)

                         JACK
            What do you say?

                         COLLEGE KID
            I dunno -- you mean it?

                         JACK
            Anything you wanna do -- you do it.
            Do you see this young lady here?

                         COLLEGE KID
              Yeah.

                         JACK
            You like what you see?

                         COLLEGE KID
              Sure.

                         JACK
            Then get in here and do what you want.

       The College Kid gets in the car, sits next to Rollergirl, who nods
       hello. She may or may not recoginize him. Jack gets in the seat
       opposite (behind the CAMERA.)

                         JACK
            You a student?

                         COLLEGE KID
            Uh...um...yeah.

                         JACK
            Oh, great. Where do you go to school?

                         COLLEGE KID
            Um...uh...do I have to say?

                              JACK
                    No, no. Anyway. How'd you like to go round
                    with Rollergirl, have you seen her film work?

                              COLLEGE KID
                    ...yeah...yeah I have.
                              (to Rollegirl)
                    We watch your films in my frat house.
                    I go to CSUN. The fuckin' guys are never
                    gonna believe this --

                              JACK
                    Alright...fantastic cool...

                              COLLEGE KID
                    I think we met once before, actually.

                              ROLLERGIRL
                    Really?

          BEAT.

                              COLLEGE KID
                    I know you....we went to school together.
                    We went to high school together.
                    .....you're Brandy, right? Brandy's your name.

          Rollergirl looks caught. Jack looks suprised to hear this...

                                                        CUT TO:

    161   EXT. STUDIO CITY/ALLEY-WAY - NIGHT (LATER)   161

          Dirk is standing in an alley-way. HEADLIGHTS FLOAT ACROSS A WALL,
          CATCHING A GLIMPSE OF DIRK. A small Toyota drives up and stops next
          to Dirk. A FIGURE inside the car speaks;

                              FIGURE
                    Hello.

                              DIRK
                    Hey.

                              FIGURE
                    Are you waiting for someone?

                              DIRK
                    ...yeah. I'm waiting for someone.
                    I'm not sure if they're gonna show up though.

                              FIGURE
                    You wanna wait in the car?

          BEAT. Dirk gets into the Toyota. It drives about fifty yards
          down the alley and makes a turn into --

162 EXT. EMPTY PARKING LOT - NIGHT - THAT MOMENT   162

The Toyota with Dirk pulls around and parks.

CUT TO:

163 INT. TOYOTA - PARKED - NIGHT - THAT MOMENT   163

CAMERA holds a profile 2-shot on Dirk in the f.g. and the driver
in the b.g. The driver is a young SURFER kid in his late 20s.

                         SURFER
               I'm Joe.

                         DIRK
               Dirk.
                         (beat)
               Do you know who I am?

                         SURFER
               ....No....

                         DIRK
               My name is Dirk Diggler.

                         SURFER
               No...I mean...you're a guy...I'm
               helping you out....

                         DIRK
               Yeah.

                         SURFER
               So....what do you want to do?

                         DIRK
               I'm...it's what you want.

                         SURFER
               ....I wanna watch you. I mean, I'm not gay.
               I just wanna. Maybe you can jerk off
               a little and I can watch. Maybe I'll join
               in, but for now I just wanna watch.

Dirk nods his head a little. HOLD.

                         DIRK
               Twenty bucks.

                         SURFER
               Ten is all I have....

                                                        CUT TO:

INT. LIMO - MOVING - MOMENTS LATER

The limo is moving now. Jack is sitting behind the CAMERA.
The LIGHT held above the Camcorder SHINES brightly on them.

Rollergirl and the College Kid struggle in the seat. He has some
trouble removing his pants and she tries to help a little, but it's
pretty she's not enjoying this. Jack tries to coach them from the
sidelines;

                         JACK
               Alright, there, pal; make it look
               good, make it sexy -- don't just ram
               your way up and in there --

The College Kid doesn't respond.

                         JACK
               Hey, hey, hey....take it slow and
               make it kinky, kid. C'mon.
               Think of Miss Lovely Rollergirl
               as a beautiful instrument that you
               need to play...c'mon now...slow down...
               Pretend you're just a wonderful stud,
               pretend you're a wonderful stud that's
               just ready melt her pussy....hey, kid....?
               Are you listening to me? Hey -- Hey --

                      COLLEGE KID
               Just lemme do my thing, man.

                         JACK
               Cut. Stop. Cut.

The College Kid looks a little pissed, Rollergirl pushes him off;

                      ROLLERGIRL
               This is stupid, Jack.

                         JACK
               I know....this isn't working out.

                      COLLEGE KID
               That's it?

                      JACK (OC)
               Yeah, that's all. Sorry for the inconvenience.

The College Kid pulls his pants on.

                      COLLEGE KID
               You got me hard -- you could at least
               jack me off or something, lady.

                      ROLLERGIRL
               What the fuck did you say?

                    COLLEGE KID
              It's not so cool to leave me
              with a hard on.

                    ROLLERGIRL
              Fuck you.

                    COLLEGE KID
              Nice life you've got here. Should
              be proud of what you've become...

The College Kid laughs a little, heads out of the car, turns back
to Jack and says:

                    COLLEGE KID
              You're fuckin' films suck now anyway.

ANGLE, CU. JACK.
CAMERA DOLLIES IN A LITTLE IN SLOW MOTION. He freaks out.

Jack CHARGES out of the limo TACKLING the College Kid to the ground.
He starts to BEAT the shit out him....

                                                    CUT TO:

165   INT. TOYOTA - PARKED - THAT MOMENT   165

Dirk zips his pants open. The Surfer kid's eyes watch closely.
Dirk pulls out his cock and the Surfer kid looks surprised,
speaks sotto;

                    SURFER
              ...holy shit...that's nice...that's...big...

Dirk nods, looks down.

                    SURFER
              Why don't you jerk it a little,
              get it hard? I wanna see it get hard.

Dirk's hand touches his cock and he starts to masturbate a little.
The Surfer kid watches. CAMERA BEGINS A PAINFULLY SLOW ZOOM INTO
PROFILE XCU. ON DIRK.

                    SURFER
              ...maybe...do it harder....

Dirk does it harder and faster.

                    SURFER
              Get your hand wet.

                    DIRK
              ...be quiet....

Dirk tries to do it faster and harder.

                              SURFER
                    ...c'mon....c'mon...c'mon...

Dirk tries harder and faster but only gets more frustrated.
He verges on tears, looks to the Surfer Kid.

                              DIRK
                    I can't...I can't get it hard...I can't.
                    I'm sorry --

SUDDENLY:
A PICK-UP TRUCK carrying THREE PUNK KIDS SLAMS ON IT'S BRAKES
IN FRONT OF DIRK IN THE TOYOTA. Dirk looks up in shock, turns his
head to the Surfer Kid who says;

                              SURFER
                    You shouldn't do this sort of thing, faggot.

Surfer PUNCHES Dirk in the face....

                                                       CUT TO:

166   EXT. VENTURA BLVD. - NIGHT - THAT MOMENT   166

       Jack continues to BEAT the College Kid and yell at him;

                              JACK
                    YOU HAVE SOME FUCKING RESPECT.
                    YOU LITTLE PRICK. YOU HAVE SOME GOD DAMN
                    RESPECT FOR THAT GIRL. SHE'S A STAR,
                    A WONDERFUL CHILD AND A STAR. You think
                    you're worthy to fuck her - you're not
                    worthy to TOUCH her - they way you fuck -
                    who taught you? WHO TAUGHT YOU HOW TO FUCK
                    THAT WAY? YOU'RE AN AMATUER. AN AMATUER.

       He KICKS the College Kid again and again...CAMERA DOLLIES
       IN ON ROLLERGIRL as she watches. She rolls over....stands
       a BEAT over the College Kid....and then goes crazy....she SMASHES
       his face with her ROLLERSKATES over and over and over;

                              ROLLERGIRL
                    YOU - DON'T - EVER - DISRESPECT - ME.

       She breaks down CRYING and SCREAMING....Jack pulls her off....

                                                       CUT TO:

167   EXT. PARKING LOT - THAT MOMENT   167

       The FOUR SURFER PUNKS drag Dirk from the car and proceed to beat
       the shit out of him. Kicking and punching him, calling out;

                              SURFERS
                    Little Fuckin Fag. Donkey-Dick.
                    You don't do this. You don't.

They continue to yell and scream and kick and punch Dirk
and eventually peel out of the parking lot. Dirk moans and cries and
holds his stomach in pain. He coughs up some blood and vomit....

CAMERA PANS away from him, looking out of the alley way, towards
Ventura Blvd.. HOLD WIDE ANGLE ON THE STREET, EMPTY FRAME, THEN;

The WHITE LIMO carrying Jack and Rollergirl cruises PAST.

ANGLE, IN THE STREET, MOMENT LATER.
The WHITE LIMO drives PAST CAMERA LFT. HOLD, THEN; BUCK'S CAR
enters in CAMERA RT. and we PICK UP AND PAN with it into --

                                                CUT TO:

168   EXT. DONUT SHOP/VENTURA BLVD. - NIGHT   168

Buck's car pulls up and parks in front of the donut shop. CAMERA
DOLLIES IN CLOSE. Jessie is in the passenger seat, Buck leaves the
engine running;

                    BUCK
            What do you want, honey?

                    JESSIE ST. VINCENT
            I want...um...apple fritter...Jelly....
            and uh....chocolate with sprinkles...and
            a bear claw, too....

Buck gets out of the car and we reveal that she is SIX MONTHS
PREGNANT. Buck looks down;

                    BUCK
            How's my little kung-fu fighter?

                    JESSIE ST. VINCET
            He's kicking ass inside my stomach.

                    BUCK
            That's a boy.

                                                CUT TO:

169   INT. DONUT SHOP - NIGHT   169

Buck enters and looks at some donuts, helped by the DONUT BOY behind
the counter. A MIDDLE AGED MAN in a camouflage baseball hat sits in
the corner eating a donut and some coffee, reading 'Guns and Ammo.'

                    DONUT BOY
            Can I help you?

                    BUCK
            Yeah....I'm gonna get a dozen....

The Donut Boy gets a box and Buck starts to point out;

                                BUCK
          Lemme get two bear claws...apple fritter...
          two chocolate....two sprinkles...gimme
          some of those glazed...how many is that?

At that moment a PUERTO RICAN KID walks in, pulls a REVOLVER
from his pocket and points at the Donut Boy.

                         PUERTO RICAN KID
          Empty the safe. Behind the soda machine.

                                BUCK
          Jesus Christ.

The Puerto Rican Kid SWINGS HIS AIM at Buck.

                         PUERTO RICAN KID
          Don't talk...shut the fuck up...
                    (aims back at Donut Boy)
          Okay...empty the safe....

Donut Boy starts to empty the safe, putting the money
in a paper sack....Buck is frozen....

The MIDDLE AGED MAN in the corner reaches into his coat pocket
and pulls out an extremely BIG GUN...

The Middle Aged Man SHOOTS the Puerto Rican Kid in the BACK...

...the Puerto Rican Kid turns and returns FIRE, hitting the Middle
Aged Man with a bullett in the FACE...

....the Middle Aged Man gets another wild SHOT off before he expires
and that bullett hits the Donut Boy in the CHEST....

So: The Donut Boy is dead, The Puerto Rican Kid falls to the floor
dead and the Middle Aged Man is face down dead in his donut and
coffee....

Blood is ALL OVER Buck......he stands for a long moment....

CU. THE BAG OF MONEY ON THE FLOOR

CU. BUCK.
he looks at it. SLOW ZOOM IN. BEAT.

Buck leans down, picks up the BAG FULL OF MONEY and walks out
of the donut shop.

                                              FADE OUT.

TITLE CARD, OVER BLACK: "One Last Thing"

INT. EL PUEBLO MOTEL ROOM - NIGHT

Reed, Todd and Dirk sit around a table. Dirk is bandaged.
Scotty J. is mingling around in the background. CAMERA DOES
A SLOW 360 AROUND THE TABLE.

                    TODD
          Alright. I think this could be the thing.
          Something to help us score a little extra cash.
          I think if we decide to do this, we gotta be
          one hundred percent.

               REED
          I agree.

                    TODD
          This guys name is Rahad Jackson.
          He's got more money than God and twice
          as much coke, crack and smack. He'll buy
          just about anything anybody wants to sell him.
          He just likes people hanging out at his house
          and partying.

                    DIRK
          How do you know him?

                    TODD
          He used to come into Party Boys
          once in a while. Mutrix introduced me --

                    DIRK
          And how would we do it, exactly?
          I mean, how would it all go down?

                    TODD
          It's like this: I call him up,
          tell him if got half of key of quality stuff.

                    REED
          Do you have his phone number?

                    TODD
          Yeah. So we call him up, give him the price?

                    DIRK
          How much?

                    TODD
          Half a key for like....five thousand bucks.
          Split it three ways --

                    DIRK
          That's enough to get my Vette fixed.

                        TODD
          That's right. So we set up the deal,
          dump half a kilo of baking soda in a
          bag and walk over to his house -- BOOM.
          Right there -- this could be a nifty bit
          'o hustle-bustle.

                        REED
          Do you have his adress?

                        TODD
          Fuckin', Reed, yeah I have his adress, c'mon.

                        DIRK
          What if he tests it out?

                        TODD
          He won't.

                        DIRK
          How do you know?

                        TODD
          I know he won't. I'm positive. Believe me.

                        REED
          It's a pretty good idea.

                        DIRK
          I think we should go for it.

          Scotty J. comes over to the table.

                        SCOTTY J.
          You guys should be careful with this.

                        DIRK
          Scotty?

                        SCOTTY J.
          What?

                        DIRK
          Just...y'know...mind yer own business.

                        SCOTTY J.
          Sorry.

          ECU - Baking soda poured in a plastic bag.
          ECU - The plastic bag wrapped in a brown paper sack.
          ECU - Dirk's car keys grabbed off the table.

                                        CUT TO:

The Corvette pulls up in front of a tacky-one story house in
the hills of Studio City. The Corvette stops and CAMERA DOLLIES
IN QUICK. Dirk, Reed, Todd sit in the parked car. In sotto;

                    DIRK
          Okay.

                    TODD
          You guys ready for this?

                    REED
          I am.

                    TODD
          Dirk?

                    DIRK
          Me? Yeah...yeah I'm ready. I was born ready.

                    TODD
          Alright.

Todd takes out a .45 AUTOMATIC PISTOL and loads a cartridge.

                    DIRK
          What the fuck is that?

                    TODD
          It's a big gun.

                    DIRK
          I know-but-why?

                    TODD
          Just in case, just in case. Let's go.

They pile out of the damaged Corvette and walk up. CAMERA (STEADICAM)
follows them.

                    REED
          I'm nervous.

                    TODD
          It'll be okay.

                    REED
          Let's get in and out, in and out.

                    TODD
          Not too quick -- that looks suspicious.
          Lemme do the talking --

They arrive and ring the doorbell.

                                        CUT TO:

A really big fat black BODYGUARD comes to the door and opens up:

> BODYGUARD
> Hello. Come on in.

The BodyGuard leads them down a hall and into a tacky and spacious, sunken LIVING ROOM.

. They're greeted by a man in a silk robe, slightly open to show some bikini briefs and a thin sheen of sweat covering his body:
RAHAD JACKSON (late 40s)

Off in a corner of the room, a YOUNG ASIAN KID is casually throwing some FIRECRACKERS around.

Rahad is DANCING around by himself to NIGHT RANGER, "SISTER CHRISTIAN." He spots the men;

> RAHAD
> Hello, friends. Which one is Todd?

> TODD
> That's me. We met before at the club --

> RAHAD
> Oh, yeah. Come on in here.

> TODD
> These are my friends Dirk and Reed.

> RAHAD
> Great to meet you. You guys want something
> to drink -- or a pill -- or some coke --
> or some dope?

> DIRK/REED/TODD
> No thank you, thanks, no.

> RAHAD
> So what do we have, we have, something, yeah?

> TODD
> Here it is...half a key...it's really good,
> if you wanna test it out --

> RAHAD
> Oh, wait a minute, I love this part:
>   (sings along)
> "SISTER CHRISTIAN, THERE'S SO MUCH
> IN LIFE, DON'T YOU GIVE IT UP BEFORE
> YOUR TIME IS DUE....IT'S TRUE!"
>   (to Dirk)
> This song is so amazing.
> Anyway; What's the price?

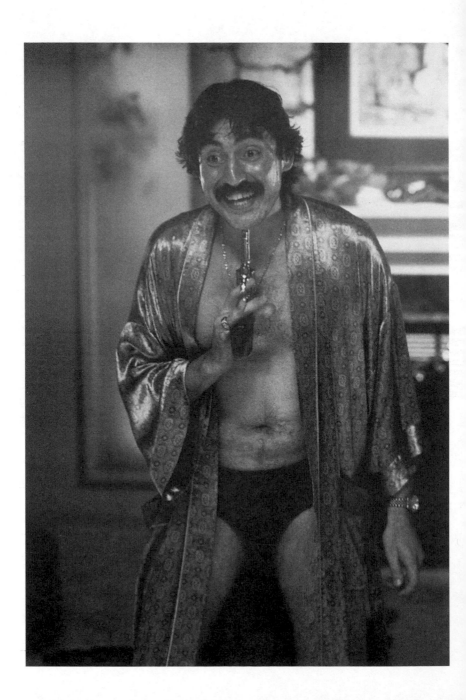

                              TODD
              We were thinking five thousand.

                              RAHAD
              That's good. No problem, cool, cool.

The Bodyguard brings over a PAPER BAG FULL OF CASH and hands the
bag to Todd in exchange for the PAPER BAG FULL OF BAKING SODA.

Reed watches the Bodyguard take the bag and notices something.
REED'S POV: a SHOULDER HOLSTER holds a .45 Automatic Pistol.

Rahad does an air guitar solo to the the Night Ranger song....he walks
across the room, picks up a COKE PIPE and looks to the guys;

                              RAHAD
              You wanna play baseball?

                          DIRK/REED/TODD
              No thank you.

Rahad smokes the pipe while dancing. Dirk looks across to an open
bedroom door.

DIRK'S POV: Through the crack in the door, we can see a bloody,
battered YOUNG BLACK WOMAN in a silk robe....she's followed by
another YOUNG WHITE GIRL in nothing.

                          RAHAD (OC)
              Check this out --

He takes out a nickel plated REVOLVER and loads a single bullet,
spins the chamber and puts it to his head and sings;

                              RAHAD
              SISTER CHRISTIAN - OH THE TIME HAS
              COME....AND YOU KNOW THAT YOU'RE
              THE ONLY ONE TO SAY...OK....

He pulls the trigger....Click...he smiles and casually speaks;

                              RAHAD
              I put a mix tape together of all
              my favorite songs....This is song number
              three...I love putting mix tapes together,
              you know...if you buy an album or tape or
              something, those guys put the songs in their
              order and they try and say how you should listen
              to the songs, but I don't like that.
              I don't like to be told what to listen
              to, when to listen to or anything...

The Night Ranger song FADES OUT....BEAT.....Rahad smiles at
the Asian Kid who's casually throwing some firecrackers around.

                         RAHAD
                    (to Dirk/Reed/Todd)
          He's Chinese...he loves to set off
          firecrackers.....

REO SPEEDWAGON, "CAN'T FIGHT THIS FEELING," begins to play.

                         RAHAD
          I CAN'T FIGHT THIS FEELING ANY LONGER
          AND YET I'M STILL AFRAID TO LET IT FLOW.
          WHAT STARTED OUT AS FRIENDSHIP HAS GROWN
          STRONGER -- I ONLY WISH I HAD THE STRENGTH
          TO LET IT SHOW --

                         DIRK
          Well...I think maybe....we better get going --

                         RAHAD
          No, stay. Hang out. We'll party.

                         DIRK
          No, we really gotta split.
          We have to be somewhere and we --

Dirk and Rahad continue to haggle about leaving/not leaving.
CAMERA BEGINS A SLOW DOLLY INTO A CU ON TODD.

                         TODD
          We're Not Leaving Yet.

Dirk and Reed look at Todd. He stands up.

                         TODD
          We're here now and we want something else.
          Hey -- Hey. We Want Something Else From You.

                         RAHAD
          What?

                         DIRK
          Todd -- what the hell are you doing?

                         TODD
          In the master bedroom, under the bed,
          in a floor safe....You understand?

The Bodyguard turns his head. Dirk and Reed are confused;

                         DIRK
          Todd...what the fuck, man, c'mon --

                         TODD
          Shut-up, Dirk.   I told you I got a plan.
          I got a good plan.

                         RAHAD
          Are you kiddn' me kittie?

                    TODD
          No I'm not. I'm not kidding. We want
          what's in the safe. We want what's in
          the safe in the floor under the bed in
          the master bedroom.

                    DIRK
          Todd -- don't be crazy.
                    (to Rahad)
          Sir -- we don't know anything about this.
          This is not the thing that we wanted.

                    TODD
          SHUT THE FUCK UP, DIRK.

The BODYGUARD reaches into his coat...

...Todd pulls his REVOLVER quickly and AIMS at the BodyGuard.

                    TODD
          Don't reach for your gun.

...Rahad reacts by AIMING HIS GUN AT TODD...

                    RAHAD
          You don't wanna do this, friendly.

                    TODD
          You've only got one bullet.

Rahad PULLS THE TRIGGER...a bullett FIRES from the gun and
strikes Todd in the SHOULDER...the gun in his hand falls to
the floor and he stumbles back...

...The Bodyguard takes this moment to GRAB HIS OWN GUN from the
holster and FIRE off shots at DIRK and REED....

...Bullets graze past them and they DUCK FOR COVER...

...The GIRLS in the bedroom SCREAM and SHOUT at the gunfire...

...a STRAY BULLET HITS the ASIAN KID in the heart, but he
doesn't fall...

...TODD reaches hold of his gun, crouches for cover and FIRES
a bullet STRAIGHT INTO the Bodyguard...who falls back DEAD....Todd
looks right and sees:

RAHAD scuttles into the bedroom with the women....Todd looks
over his shoulder to Dirk and Reed;

                    DIRK
          WHAT THE FUCK ARE YOU DOING, TODD?

                    TODD
          He went in the bedroom.

                    DIRK
        ARE YOU CRAZY? WHEN DID YOU GO CRAZY?

                    TODD
        He's got cash and coke in the safe
        under the bed -- if we leave here
        without it we're fools.

                    REED
        Let's just split, let's just split
        right now, Todd. Don't be stupid.
        This wasn't part of the deal.

                    TODD
        I'm goin' in that bedroom and get what's
        in that safe. Are you coming?

                    DIRK
        Fuck no. Todd. Don't. Don't do it.

Todd gets up and heads for the bedroom with his revolver at the
ready....he inches closer to the door and twists the door knob,
then KICKS THE DOOR OPEN;

...<u>Rahad is standing right there</u>, holding a SAWED OFF SHOTGUN.
He pulls the trigger....Todd blinks....

...Rahad's SHOTGUN BLAST blows Todd BACK and UP in the air
about fifteen feet....he FALLS to the ground with a HOLE in his
STOMACH the size of a basketball...Rahad calls out to Dirk and Reed;

                    RAHAD
        C'mon out little puppies. You want to
        come and see, come and see, to get what
        is coming down. <u>Coming down</u>.

Rahad peers out from his bedroom, sees a sliver of Dirk behind
the wall. Rahad FIRES HIS SHOTGUN...which cuts right past
Dirk's head and SHREDS the wall near him....

Reed and Dirk make a DASH for the front door....

...Rahad FIRES another shot...

...a BLAST BREEZES PAST THEIR HEADS....

Dirk and Reed make it OUTSIDE....Rahad chases after them.....

                                        CUT TO:

174 EXT. RAHAD'S HOUSE - THAT MOMENT   174

     Reed and Dirk make a dash for the Corvette -- they're steps away
     when a SHOTGUN BLAST BLOWS INTO THE PASSENGER'S SIDE DOOR --

     Reed heads away from the car -- makes a run diagonally across the
     street for shelter behind some SHRUBS and TREES -- (he gets lost from
     CAMERA)

     Dirk gets around to the driver's side of the Corvette, shielded
     and crouched -- he opens the door and starts to get in --

     ANOTHER SHOT BLOWS THE PASSENGER'S SIDE WINDOW OUT.

     GLASS SPRAYS IN HIS EYES AND HIS HAND SLIPS DOWN, RELEASING THE
     EMERGENCY BRAKE OF THE CAR -- WHICH BEGINS TO ROLL DOWN THE STREET --

     Dirk stumbles back from the car. He looks to the house:

     Rahad is about to FIRE the shotgun again....

     ....he looks down the street: the Corvette is ROLLING away and
     picking up speed as it goes down the hill --

     Dirk gets on his feet and makes a run for the car, Rahad FIRES...

     ...Dirk catches up with the car, hops in -- gets the key in the
     ignition and starts it up, peels off down the street --

                                                            CUT TO:

175 INT. DIRK'S CORVETTE - MOMENTS LATER   175

     Dirk pulls around and stops a moment. He looks around -- he looks
     back in his rearview mirror.

                              DIRK
                    Fuck -- Fuck -- Fuck.

                                                            CUT TO:

176 EXT. STREET NEARBY - THAT MOMENT   176

     Reed is running FULL-SPEED down a residential street, in and
     out of back yards and over fences, dodging attack dogs, etc.

                                                            CUT TO:

177 INT. RAHAD JACKSON'S HOUSE - THAT MOMENT   177

     RAHAD storms around his house, the SHOTGUN in his hand. The two
     battered YOUNG WOMEN are shaking and shivering in a corner --

                              RAHAD
                    What the fuck...what the fuck...what the fuck.

Rahad rants and raves incoherently, sets down the shotgun for
a moment to take a hit from his crack pipe. A DISCO song is
playing LOUDLY and Rahad is dancing. HOLD, THEN:

ANGLE, A WALL IN THE HOUSE
a red flash hits the wall.....then a blue flash hits the wall.

ANGLE, RAHAD
he looks at the wall and sees the red-blue flash.
CAMERA DOLLIES IN ON RAHAD. He smiles.

More RED-BLUE FLASHES hit the house and the SOUNDS of POLICE
ACTION starts to BUILD....

                         RAHAD
              It's coming down, <u>coming down</u>.

...RAHAD PICKS UP THE SHOTGUN, SMASHES THE WINDOW AND FIRES
OFF A SHOT TOWARDS THE OC POLICE ACTION...

...OC POLICE FIRE BACK ABOUT ONE MILLION BULLETS THAT RIP INTO
RAHAD, SENDING HIM BACK, STUMBLING ACROSS THE HOUSE, FURTHER
AND FURTHER....BULLETS RIP INTO THE TWO GIRLS, KILLING THEM.

OVERHEAD ANGLE, STRAIGHT DOWN:
Rahad's dead body fall's next to Todd's dead body...a BEAT later,
the Asian Kid finally falls over, face down next to them....

                              QUICK FADE OUT, CUT TO:

178 <u>OMITTED</u>   178

179 <u>OMITEED</u>   179

180 <u>INT. DIRK'S CORVETTE - MOVING - NIGHT</u>   180

     HOLD CU. ON DIRK. He's driving fast. Paranoid and freaked.
     The car starts to sputter....slows.....Dirk panics when he sees
     the gas tank....ECU. The Gas Tank Display. The orange needle is
     on, "E."

                                   CUT TO:

     TITLE CARD: "Fourteen Miles Later"

                                   CUT TO:

181 <u>EXT. STREET/OUTSIDE LOS ANGELES - DAWN (LATER)</u>   181 *

     Dirk's car is out of gas. He pushes the car off the main boulevard
     and down a side street.

                                   CUT TO:

EXT. SIDE STREET - THAT MOMENT

Dirk pushes his car down a small cul-de-sac, hops in and pulls
the emergency brake.

He looks around a moment. HOLD. CAMERA DOLLIES IN CLOSE ON
HIS FACE. He looks at the street signs.

OVERHEAD ANGLE, INTERSECTION.
Dirk walks to the middle of the intersection and looks up at the
sign posts. It reads, "Troost Street."

He walks down this street, looking at the houses. He walks a full two
blocks down, stops, looks: He's standing in front of his PARENTS
HOUSE. It looks just the same.

A young PAPERBOY rides past and throws the paper, hitting Dirk in the
head. He hesitates, then walks up the steps;

CAMERA MOVES IN SLOWLY ON THE DOOR, LANDS IN A CU. OVER HIS SHOULDER.
He knocks. Moments later...the door opens; A young woman in a
bathrobe with a BABY on her hip opens the door. This is SHERYL LYNN,
who we met earlier.

                         SHERYL LYNN
          Yes?

                         DIRK
          ....hello.

                         SHERYL LYNN
          Can I help you?

BEAT.

                         SHERYL LYNN
          Eddie...? Eddie.

Dirk hesitates a moment, then recognizes Sheryl Lynn.

                         DIRK
          ...what are doing here? Where's my mother?

                         SHERYL LYNN
          Eddie....I can't believe it...

                         DIRK
          ...I'm looking for my mother...
          I'm looking for my father and mother.

                         SHERYL LYNN
          Eddie, honey....my God...you just...

                         DIRK
          Why are you in this house? I don't
          want to see you, I want my mother.

                         SHERYL LYNN
              I live here, now. With my husband.

                         DIRK
              Where's my mom?

                         SHERYL LYNN
              You should come in --

BEAT. HOLD CU. ON DIRK.

                         DIRK
              No....no. Jesus Christ, I know what
              you're gonna say --

                         SHERYL LYNN
              Eddie, I can tell you what happened,
              just let me tell you inside here --

                         DIRK
              Just tell me. Just tell me.

                         SHERYL LYNN
              They passed...last May --

The baby starts to cry. Dirk doesn't move;

                         DIRK
              ...how...?

                         SHERYL LYNN
              Eddie, come inside right now, please.

                         DIRK
              YOU TELL ME, LADY.

                         SHERYL LYNN
              There was no way to find you, to get
              in touch with you. To tell you all these things --

                         DIRK
              TELL ME RIGHT NOW, YOU.

                         SHERYL LYNN
              Eddie, it was out of the blue   *
              and there was a man and he was speeding and
              he was drunk and they didn't --

                                        FLASH ON:

183   EXT. INTERSECTION - DAY   183 *

      A little Station Wagon enters the intersection   *
      with the right of way but is IMMEDIATELY AND POWERFULLY
      CRUNCHED by a SPEEDING MALIBU that barrels into the intersection.

The STATION WAGON is THROWN fifty yards away. A HORN blows...

CAMERA DOES A SLOW DOLLY IN TOWARDS THE STATION WAGON.
Dirk's MOTHER and FATHER are SOAKED IN BLOOD.

CAMERA DOES A SLOW DOLLY IN TOWARDS THE SPEEDING MALIBU.
Half in/half through the windshield of this car is <u>JOHNNY DOE</u>.

QUICK FADE OUT, CUT TO:

184   <u>EXT. DIRK'S HOUSE/TORRANCE - THAT MOMENT</u>   184

Back to the scene. HOLD ON DIRK.

                    SHERYL LYNN
          It was just some drunk kid, Eddie.

                    DIRK
          -- Why do you live here?

                    SHERYL LYNN
          My husband and I bought this house.

                    DIRK
          Why? Why did you do that?

                    SHERYL LYNN
          Eddie, please --

                    DIRK
          This is my house. THIS IS MY HOUSE.
          What the fuck? What the fuck are you
          doing here? I don't want to see you,
          I need to see my mother. I want my mother.

CUT TO:

185   <u>INT. SHERYL LYNN'S HOUSE - MOMENTS LATER</u>   185

CAMERA HOLDS IN THE KITCHEN. Sheryl Lynn makes breakfast with the
baby on her hip. Her HUSBAND sits nearby in his bathrobe, watching
the situation and keeping quiet.

Dirk is on the phone in the living room. WE HEAR ONLY MUFFLED
BITS FROM HIS CONVERSATION.

                    DIRK
               (into phone)
          ....Scotty. It's Dirk...yeah...yeah...
          lemme talk to him....Reed...yeah. yeah.
               (beat)
          are you sure....? Yeah, okay...in a little...

Dirk hangs up, looks at Sheryl Lynn and her husband.

                    SHERYL LYNN
          Is everything alright?

Dirk nods. She sets him up with a cup of coffee.

                         SHERYL LYNN
             You made something of yourself, Eddie.

She smiles, nods, points to the living room.

                         SHERYL LYNN
             I have all of your tapes...I've seen
             all of your films....I knew you'd do
             something special with it....

Dirk looks and sees that she has a collection of about 100 videotapes
on a shelf...the Husband looks a little depressed...the Baby cries....
DOLLY IN A LITTLE ON DIRK.

                                                    CUT TO:

186   INT. JACK'S HOUSE - MORNING (LATER)   186

      CAMERA holds on the hallway that looks towards the front door.
      It opens slowly and Dirk steps inside. He takes his sunglasses
      off and stands a moment.

      OC we hear some noises coming from the kitchen. Sounds of someone
      cooking something. The SOUND from the television.

      A few moments pass and Jack enters the HALLWAY and FRAME.
      Jack and Dirk stand a moment, looking at each other in silence.
      Dirk looks down, fiddles with his sunglasses, looses it;

                         DIRK
             Can you please help me?

      HOLD.
                                                    CUT TO:

187   INT. JACK'S OFFICE - DAY - MOMENTS LATER   187

      Dirk has broken down in Jack's arms. Jack hugs him and pets
      his head. AMBER enters, brings Dirk a glass of water and
      sits next to them on the couch. CAMERA DOLLIES IN SLOW.

                         JACK
             It's alright, boy. It's alright.

                                                    FADE OUT.

EXT. DOORWAY - DAY

CAMERA holds on a doorway. Buck steps out, dressed in a BREAK
DANCER outfit, looks INTO CAMERA:

                        BUCK
              Did I hear somebody say DEALS?

CAMERA CONTINUES BACK TO REVEAL the store front of "BUCK'S SUPER COOL
STEREO STORE," with a huge banner that reads, "Grand Opening."

                        BUCK
              This weekend and this weekend only
              Buck's Super Cool Stereo World is making
              Super-Cool Deals on ALL name brands.

REVERSE ANGLE: AMBER and KURT LONGJOHN are standing next to
a VIDEO CAMERA, filming a COMMERCIAL for Buck's store.

                        BUCK
              We're open, we're ready -- all you
              need to do is walk over, get down and
              come inside us --

                        AMBER
              Cut. Excellent.

                                              CUT TO:

189   INT. HIGH SCHOOL CLASSROOM - DAY   189

CAMERA DOLLIES IN ON ROLLERGIRL. She's sitting at a desk, deep
in the middle of taking the GED test. She starts to drift, looking
out the window....then back to the test.

                                              CUT TO:

190   INT. BAKERSFIELD RETIREMENT HOME - DAY   190

CAMERA DOLLIES IN ON BECKY. She's wearing a UNIFORM and working with
a group of OLD FOLKS in the retirement home. She feeds Mr. Brown
some soup and smiles.

                                              CUT TO:

191   INT. JAIL CELL - NIGHT   191

THE COLONEL sits in a jail cell with a large black man, TRYONE.

                        COLONEL
              Tyrone?

                        TYRONE
              Yes, Colonel.

                        COLONEL
              Tell me.

                         TYRONE
                You know that I love you.

                         COLONEL
                I like hearing you say it.

                         TYRONE
                You're my bitch. You always will be.

        BEAT. CAMERA DOLLIES IN ON THE COLONEL. He smiles.

                                                        CUT TO:

192   EXT. HOT TRAXX NIGHTCLUB - DAY   192

        MAURICE is standing out front with his two BROTHERS who are
        fresh off the boat....they're unveiling a new sign in front
        of the club -- the sheet drops to reveal;

        "RODRIGUEZ BROTHERS NIGHTCLUB"

                                                        CUT TO:

193   INT. NIGHTCLUB/CABARET - NIGHT   193

        CAMERA moves across the small audience to the stage where REED
        is doing a MAGIC SHOW. He's wearing a leotard and floating
        some brass rings in mid-air. He snaps his fingers and they
        drop into his hands -- he takes a bow and does a little dance.

                                                        CUT TO:

194   INT. HOSPITAL/DELIVERY ROOM - DAY   194

        CAMERA is HAND-HELD as JESSIE ST. VINCENT is screaming and
        kicking her way through labour. BUCK is holding her hand.
        SCOTTY J. is with them, filming the whole thing with a VIDEO CAMERA.

                              BUCK
                C'mon, honey, c'mon, c'mon, c'mon.

                         JESSIE ST. VINCENT
                JESUS MOTHER FUCKING CHRIST ALMIGHTY HELL.

        We hear a BABY pop out, kicking and screaming.

                              DOCTOR
                Yes, yes, Jessie. It's a boy.

                                                        CUT TO:

        End Sequence "E"

195 <u>EXT. JACK'S DRIVEWAY - DAY</u>   (June 84)   195

An EQUIPMENT TRUCK backs up towards CAMERA. ROCKY, SCOTTY J.
and KURT LONGJOHN enter FRAME and lift the back up to reveal;
A whole SET of VIDEO EQUPIMENT. They begin to unload it...

STEADICAM PULLS BACK and Jack enters FRAME, smiling and walking
back into the house...this is one continuos shot...as he moves
through, interacting with:

MAURICE is cooking some stuff up in the kitchen. Smoke everywhere.

                    JACK
          Maurice, honey, turn the fan on.

                    MAURICE
          It smells good, though.

                    JACK
          It's stinkin up the whole house.

ROLLERGIRL is skating around, listening to headphones.

                    JACK
          Rollergirl, honey, please, I just had
          the floors re-done.

                    ROLLERGIRL
          What?

                    JACK
          Your skates on the wood floor, please.

                    ROLLERGIRL
          What?

                    JACK
          Are you going deaf? Turn the music down --

                    ROLLERGIRL
          Jack, I can't hear a word you're saying.

BUCK is setting up a new audio/video system in Jack's living room.
He explains some technical information about the new format of
"compact discs."

                    JACK
          Just do me a favor and make it work, Buck.

                    BUCK
          Did I talk to you about the modification
          you're gonna need?

                    JACK
          Don't. Don't do it, Buck.

                         BUCK
              Jack - you stick with the bass
              you got and it's not gonna be loud.

                         JACK
              I don't listen to it loud, alright?
              I just wanna hear something, okay?

   Jack continues out to the POOL AREA. REED is swimming with the BABY.
   · JESSIE ST. VINCENT is doing an OIL PAINTING of them.

                         JACK
              Look at this, he's a swimmer!

                         JESSIE ST. VINCENT
                         (to the baby)
              Cna you say hello to your Uncle Jack?

                         JACK
                         (to Jessie)
              He's not gonna piss in the pool is he?

                         JESSIE ST. VINCENT
              I don't think so.

   JACK walks back in the house, down the hallway, CAMERA PANS
   to a PICTURE on the wall of LITTLE BILL then PANS back to Jack,
   who continues down the hall into --

   AMBER'S BEDROOM.
   She's sitting in front of her make-up table. He sits next to her;

                         AMBER
              Are we ready?

                         JACK
              Plenty of time.

                         AMBER
              What are you looking at?

                         JACK
              I'm looking at you, my darling.

                         AMBER
              You're staring.

   BEAT. He leans in, gives her a kiss on the cheek and says;

                         JACK
              You're the foxiest bitch I've ever known.

                                        CUT TO:

Dirk is sitting in a jean costume, script in front of him for
the new film, working on the lines. He's cleaned up a bit,
hair slicked back. He looks in the mirror;

                    DIRK
          I've been around this block twice
          looking for something...a clue.
          I've been looking for clues and something
          led me back here....yeah...so here I am.
                    (beat)
          coulda been me the one who was at
          Ringo's place when the shit went down....
                    (beat)
          Hey....I know how it is...cause I been
          there....we've all done bad things....
          we all have those guilty feelings in
          our hearts....you wanna take your
          brain out of your head and wash it and
          scrub it and make it clean....well no.
                    (beat)
          But I'm gonna help you settle this...
                    (beat)
          First we're gonna check for holes,
          see what we can find...then we're
          gonna get nice and wet...so you're
          gonna spread your legs....
                    (beat)
          That's good...so you know me, you
          know my reputation....thirteen
          inches is a tough load, I don't
          treat you gently....That's right:
          I'm Brock Landers.
                    (beat)
          So I'm gonna be nice and I'm gonna
          ask you one more time....
                    (beat)
          Where the fuck is Ringo?

Dirk stands up, unzips his pants and let's his cock hang out.
He looks at the REFLECTION of it in the mirror;

                    DIRK
          I'm a star, I'm a star, I'm a star.
          I'm a star. I'm a star, I'm a big
          bright shinning star.

He puts his cock back in his pants, does a final karate kick and
walks out of the room, closing the door behind him.

                         END.

a PAUL THOMAS ANDERSON picture. Copyright, 1995

BOOGIE NIGHTS

Written and Directed By
PAUL THOMAS ANDERSON

Produced By
LLOYD LEVIN
JOHN LYONS
PAUL THOMAS ANDERSON
JOANNE SELLAR

Executive Producer
LAWRENCE GORDON

Co-Executive Producers
MICHAEL DE LUCA
LYNN HARRIS

Co-Producer
DANIEL LUPI

Director of Photography
ROBERT ELSWIT

Production Designer
BOB ZIEMBICKI

Editor
DYLAN TICHENOR

Costume Designer
MARK BRIDGES

Music By
MICHAEL PENN

Casting By
CHRISTINE SHEAKS

DON CHEADLE
played
Buck Swope

HEATHER GRAHAM
played
Rollergirl

LUIS GUZMAN
played
Maurice TT Rodriguez

PHILIP BAKER HALL
played
Floyd Gondolli

PHILIP SEYMOUR HOFFMAN
played
Scotty J

THOMAS JANE
played
Todd Parker

RICKY JAY
played
Kurt Longjohn

WILLIAM H. MACY
played
Little Bill

ALFRED MOLINA
played
Rahad Jackson

JULIANNE MOORE
played
Amber Waves

NICOLE ARI PARKER
played
Becky Barnett

JOHN C. REILLY
played
Reed Rothchild

BURT REYNOLDS
played
Jack Horner

ROBERT RIDGELY
played
The Colonel James

MARK WAHLBERG
played
Dirk Diggler

MELORA WALTERS
played
Jessie St. Vincent

NINA HARTLEY
played
Little Bill's Wife

MICHAEL JACE
played
Jerome

JACK WALLACE
played
Rocky

JOHN DOE
played
Amber's Husband

JOANNA GLEASON
played
Dirk's Mother

LAUREL HOLLOMAN
played
Sheryl Lynn

JONATHON QUINT
played
Johnny Doe

STANLEY DESANTIS
played
Buck's Manager

Dedicated to
ERNIE ANDERSON
(1923–1997)

Dedicated to
ROBERT RIDGELY
(1932–1997)

A LAWRENCE GORDON PRODUCTION

IN ASSOCIATION WITH GHOULARDI FILM COMPANY

A.P.T. ANDERSON PICTURE

DANIEL LUPI	Unit Production Manager
JOHN WILDERMUTH	First Assistant Director
ADAM DRUXMAN	Second Assistant Director

CAST

MAURICE T.T. RODRIGUEZ	Luis Guzman
JACK HORNER	Burt Reynolds
AMBER WAVES	Julianne Moore
HOT TRAXX WAITER	Rico Bueno
REED ROTHCHILD	John C. Reilly
BECKY BARNETT	Nicole Ari Parker
BUCK SWOPE	Don Cheadle
ROLLERGIRL	Heather Graham
EDDIE ADAMS/DIRK DIGGLER	Mark Wahlberg
LITTLE BILL	William H. Macy
HOT TRAXX CHEF	Samson Barkhordarian
LITTLE BILL'S WIFE	Nina Hartley
BIG STUD	Brad Braeden
DIRK'S MOTHER	Joanna Gleason
DIRK'S FATHER	Lawrence Hudd
STEREO CUSTOMER	Michael Stein
BUCK'S MANAGER	Stanley DeSantis
TEACHER	Patricia Forte
HIGH SCHOOL/COLLEGE KID	Kai Lennox
SHERYL LYNN	Laurel Holloman
JOHNNY LIMO DRIVER	Jason Andrews
THE COLONEL JAMES	Robert Ridgely
COLONEL'S LADY FRIEND	Amber Hunter
YOUNG STUD	Greg Lauren

WATCHER #1	Tom Dorfmeister
WATCHER #2	Jake Cross
KURT LONGJOHN	Ricky Jay
SCOTTY J.	Philip Seymour Hoffman
ROCKY	Jack Wallace
HOT TRAXX DJ	Selwyn Emerson Miller
COLONEL'S HOT TRAXX GIRLFRIEND	Jamielyn Gamboa
BECKY'S GIRLFRIEND	Melissa Spell
BECKY'S GIRLFRIEND'S FRIEND	Raymond Laboriel
JESSIE ST. VINCENT	Melora Walters
AWARDS CEREMONY BAND	Jon Brion
	Brian Kehew
	Robin Sharp
	Audrey Wiechman
RAPHAEL	Tim 'Stuffy' Soronen
JEROME	Michael Jace
FLOYD GONDOLLI	Philip Baker Hall
FLOYD'S KIDS (BOYS)	Alexander D. Slanger
	Thomas Lenk
FLOYD'S KIDS (GIRLS)	Lexi Leigh
	Laura Gronewald
TODD PARKER	Thomas Jane
MUGSY JACK'S BARTENDER	Vernon Guichard II
NEW YEAR'S EVE YOUNG STUD	Tony Tedeschi
KC SUNSHINE	Leslie Redden
MINISTER	Gregory Daniel
JOHNNY DOE	Jonathon Quint
NICK THE ENGINEER	Michael Penn
BANK WORKER	Don Amendolia
SUMMER/SKYE (JACUZZI GIRLS)	Themselves
BURT STUDIO MANAGER	Robert Downey Sr. (A Prince)
JUDGE	Veronica Hart
LAWYER	Jack Riley
AMBER'S HUSBAND	John Doe
SURFER	Cannon Roe
SURFER PUNKS	Mike Gunther
	Michael Raye Smith
	Michael Scott Stencil
DONUT BOY	Dustin Courtney
MAN WITH GUN	Allan Graf
PUERTO RICAN KID	Jose Chaidez

RAHAD'S BODYGUARD	B. Philly Johnson
RAHAD JACKSON	Alfred Molina
COSMO (RAHAD'S BOY)	Joe G. M. Chan
TYRONE	Goliath
MAURICE'S BROTHERS	Israel Juarbe
	George Anthony Rae
DOCTOR	Eric Winzenried
HOT TRAXX DANCERS	Sharon Ferrol
	Anne Fletcher
	Scott Fowler
	Melanie A. Gage
	Eddie Garcia
	Sebastian LaCause
	Lance MacDonald
	Diane Mizota
	Nathan Frederic Prevost
	Lisa E. Ratzin
	Dee Dee Weathers
	Darrel W. Wright

CREW

Executive in Charge of Production	Carla Fry
Production Executive	Leon Dudevoir
Executive in Charge of Post Production	Joe Fineman
Post Production Supervisor	Mark Graziano
Music Supervisors	Karen Rachtman
	Bobby Lavelle
Set Decorator	Sandy Struth
Art Director	Ted Berner
Sound Mixer	Stephen Halbert
Script Supervisor	Jayne Ann Tenggren
Property Master	Kevin Hughes
Production Accountant	Julie Hansen
Production Supervisor	Craig Markey
Production Coordinator	Eileen Malyszko
Unit Supervisor	Dan Collins
Steadicam/Second Camera Operator	Andy Shuttleworth
1st Assistant Camera	Michael Riba
2nd Assistant Camera	John Stradling
Camera Loader	Sean Hunter Moe

1st Assistant Editor	Joan Sobel
2nd Assistant Editor	Fred Raskin
Apprentice Editors	Danny Miller
	Bethany Orleman
Post Production Assistant	Marie Gaerlan
Casting Associate	Cassandra Kulukundis
Boom Operator	David Halbert
Utility Sound Technician	Sprocket Uporsky
Additional Sound	Peter Halbert
Chief Lighting Technician	Jeff Zucker
Best Boy	Steve Brock
Electricians	Benny Buck
	Joe Colangelo
	Keith Davis
	George Lozano
	Willie Gray
	Ngoli Nirenda
Rigging Gaffer	Jeff Orsa
Key Grip	Joseph Dianda
Best Boy Grip	Scott Patten
Dolly Grip	Kenny Davis
Grips	Nick Arnds
	R. Shawn Ensign
	Bill McDevitt
	Jamie Fronta
Assistant Property Masters	Stephen Flynn
	Suzanne Lapick
Leadman	Chris Carriveau
On Set Dresser	Martin Milligan
Swing Gang	Victor Bazaz
	Ken Carriveau
	Gregg Hartman
Set Decorating Buyer	Kristen Gassner
Assistant Art Director	Gayle Simon
Art Department Supervisor	Andrea Carter
Make-Up Supervisor	Tina K. Roesler
Assistant Make-Up Artist	Suzanne Diaz
Make-Up for Burt Reynolds	Brian K. McManus
Additional Make-Up	Eva Marie Denst
	Lynn Rodgers
Hair Supervisor	Theo Mayes
Assistant Hair	Jon Von Lingner

Additional Hair	Evelyn Rozenfeld
Assistant Costume Designer	Kimberly Adams Galligan
Costume Supervisor	David Davenport
Key Costumer	Cookie Lopez
Costumers	Linda Cormany
	Janet Stirner-Ingram
Tailor	Pablo Nantas
Seamstress	Olga Ishkhanova
Location Manager	Boyd Wilson
Assistant Location Manager	Larry Ring
Location Scouts	Dwayne Mark Alezandre
	James Lenox
	Chanel Salzer
	Joel Sinderman
	Jim Small
1st Assistant Accountant	Minnie Duerr
Payroll Accountant	Penny Gillman
Accounting Clerk	Nicole Sarrocco
Wardrobe Estimator	Marie Gaerlan
Extras Casting	Axium Casting Agency
	Rich King
Choreographer	Adam Shankman
2nd 2nd Assistant Director	Maria Battle
Set Production Assistants	Michael Phillips Jr.
	Jeff Trachtman
	Rob Montalbano
Production Secretary	Karri O'Reilly
Office Staff Assistants	Jenna DuPree
	Brad Coombs
	Liam Curtin
Unit Production Assistants	Jon Krueger
	Eric Berger
	Michael Tappan
Assistant to the Director	Jocelyne Kelly
Assistants to the Producers	Nina Grossman
	David Nickoll
	(Mark Silverman Fellow,
	The Sundance Institute)
Assistant to Burt Reynolds	Scott Jackson
Assistants to Mark Wahlberg	Eric Anthony Thomas
	Eric Weinstein
Additional Production Assistants	Gregory Donald Gately

	Jonathan Herman
	Layla Ross
Digital Sound Design & Editing	Soundswild, Inc.
Supervising Sound Editor	Dane A. Davis, MPSE
ADR Supervisor	James Borgardt
ADR Mixer	Dean St. John
ADR Recordist	Joseph Bosco
Sound Effects Editors	Kini Kay
	Mark Yardas
	John Kwiatkowski
Foley Supervisor	Valerie Davidson
Foley Editor	Tom Hammond
Dialog Editors	Charles W. Ritter
	Lou Kleinman
Music Editor	Ron Finn
Assistant Sound Editors	David McRell
	Barbara Way
Foley Artists	Laura Macias
	Sharon Michaels
	Marine Moore
	Rick Partlow
Foley Mixers	Stephen Hart
	Ron Bedrosian
Foley Recordists	Stephen Hart
	Jeremy Molod
Digital/Analog Audio Engineering	Frank Long
	Bradford Bell
Voice Casting	Barbara Harris
ADR Recorded at	4MC Company
Final Re-Recording	The Saul Zaentz Film Center
Supervising Re-Recording Mixer	David Parker
Re-Recording Mixer	Sam Lehmer
Machine Room Supervisor	Frank Canonica
Machine Room Operators	Grant Foerster
	Anna Geyer
	Dan Olmsted
Pre-Dubs Re-Recorded at	Creative Cafe Wilshire, LLC
Pre-Dub Re-Recording Mixers	Sergio Reyes
	Sebastian Tennyson
Pre-Dub Recordist	Denise Bell
Pre-Dub Re-Recording Engineers	Mike Morongel
	Ryan Robinson

Special Effects Supervisor	Lou Carlucci
Special Effects Provided by	Film Technical Services, Inc.
Special Effects Administrator	Dianne Carlucci
Special Effects	John Carlucci
	Josh Hakian
	Mick Strawn
	Adam Campbell
	Ron Myers
	Blair
Special Make-Up Effects by	K.N.B. EFX Group, Inc.
Supervisors	Robert Kurtzman
	Greg Nicotero
	Howard Berger
Crew	Garrett Immel
	James Hall
	Louis Kiss
	Robert Maverick
Coordinator	Kamar Bitar
Runner	Karrie Aubuchon
Production Controller	Paul Prokop
Product Resources	Jennifer Mosberg
In-House Coordinator	Emily Glatter
Film Services	Brent Kaviar
Rights Clearances	Clearvision
	Lana Hale
	Patrick Jager
Production Clearances	Nina Grossman
Copyright Clearances	Marshall Plumb
Assistant Choreographer	Anne Fletcher
Unit Publicity	The Pogachefsky Company
	Michael Lawson
Unit Photographer	Gillian Lefkowitz
International Publicity	Dennis Davidson Associates
Projectionist	Tom Ajar
Preview Technical Supervisor	Lee Tucker
Catering by	Sunrise Catering
Caterer	Mike Shultz
Assistant Cooks	Jose Lopez
	Arnie Lopez
Craft Service	Valeria Migliassi Collins
Set Medic	Tim Werle
Construction Coordinator	Bill Holmquist

General Foremen	Mark Balda
	David Peck
Propmakers	Richard McConnell
	Colin Alexander
	Michael Blair
	Mark Borg
	Joel Jaspan
	Greg Lay
	Greory A. Newton
	Jack Orlando
	Mark B. Palma
Lead Scenic	Patrizia Nicoloso
Painters	Greg Musselman
	Hilmar Ragnarsson
Transportation Services	Hart Transportation
Transportation Coordinator	Geno Hart
Transportation Operations Manager	Leo Stefanos
Transportation Captain	Joe Cosentino
Second Captain	Adam R. Pinkstaff
Transportation Co-Captain	Chris Waldoch
Picture Car Captain	Steve Nickolai
Drivers	Tony Barattini
	Pat Cosentino
	Angel DeSanti
	Jennifer Duclos
	Willian Dreher
	Michael Keys
	Jeff Moore
	John Pellegrino
	Randy Tenhaeff
	Steve Weible
	David Wilson
Stunt Coordinatory	Cliff Cudney
Stunts	Brian Edward Avery
	Edward L. F. Conna
	Shawn Crowder
	Gregg Dandridge
	Max Daniels
	Mark DeAlessandro
	Jeffrey Lee Gibson
	Robert McGovern
	Hugh Aodh O'Brien

	Jeff Ramsey
Police Coordinator	Ron Hughes
Security	Cast Security and On Set Security
Burt Reynolds Stand-In	Richard Bellos
Mark Wahlberg Stand-In	Chad Lane
Julianne Moore Stand-In	Andrea Nunn
Executive in Charge of Music	Toby Emmerich
Music Executives	Dana Sano, Lori Silfen
Music Clearance Executive	Mark Kaufman
Music Coordinator	Carol Dunn
Score Recorded and Mixed at	Sound Chamber
	North Hollywood, CA
Scoring Mixer	Casey Stone

SONGS

'Best of My Love'
Written by Maurice White & Al McKay
Performed by Emotions
Courtesy of Columbia Records
By arrangement with Sony Music Licensing

'Sunny'
Written by Bobby Hebb
Performed by Boney M
Courtesy of the BMG Ariola Hamburg GmbH

'Fly, Robin Fly'
Written by Stephen Prager and Sylvester Levay
Performed by Silver Convention
Courtesy of Edition Butterfly/Roswitha Kunze
By arrangement with Celebrity Licensing Inc.

'The Sage'
Written by C. Hamilton & F. Katz
Performed by Chico Hamilton Quintet
Courtesy of Blue Notes
A division of Capitol Records, Inc
Under license from EMI-Capitol Music Special Markets

'Joy'
Performed by Apollo 100
Adapted from Bach's 'Jesu, Joy of Man's Desiring'
Arranged by Tom Parker and Clive Scott
Courtesy of Start Audio & Video Ltd.
By arrangement with Celebrity Licensing Inc.

'Off the Road'
By Richard Gilks
Courtesy of Associated Production Music

'Afternoon Delight'
Written by William Danoff
Performed by Starland Vocal Band
Courtesy of Cherry Lane Music Publishing Company, Inc.
o/b/o Windsong Records

'Jungle Fever'
Written by Bill Ador
Performed by The Chakachas
Courtesy of PolyGram Records NV
By arrangement with PolyGram Film & TV Licensing

'Brand New Key'
Written by M. Safka
Performed by Melanie
Courtesy of MCA Records/BMG Entertainment International
Under license from Universal Music Special Markets and
By arrangement with BMG Entertainment

'Mama Told Me Not to Come'
Written by Randy Newman
Performed by Three Dog Night
Courtesy of MCA Records
Under license from Universal Music Special Markets

'Spill the Wine'
Written by Scott, Miller, Oskar, Jordan, Dickerson, Brown and Allen
Performed by War with Eric Burdon
Courtesy of Avenue Entertainment
By arrangement with Rhino Entertainment Company

'Lonely Boy'
Written by Andrew Gold
Performed by Andrew Gold
Courtesy of Elektra Entertainment Group
By arrangement with Warner Special Products

'Fooled Around and Fell in Love'
Written by Elvin Bishop
Performed by Elvin Bishop
Courtesy of Polydor Records
By arrangement with PolyGram Film & TV Licensing

'Fatman'
Written by Ian Anderson
Performed by Jethro Tull
Courtesy of Chrysalis Records, a division of EMI
Under license from EMI-Capitol Music Special Markets

'You Sexy Thing'
Written by Errol Brown
Performed by Hot Chocolate
Courtesy of EMI Records
Under license from EMI-Capitol Music Special Markets

'I Want to Be Free'
Written by R. Middlebrooks, J. L. Williams, M. Jones,
L. Bonner, C. Satchell, W. Beck & M. R. Pierce
Performed by Ohio Players
Courtesy of Mercury Records
By arrangement with PolyGram Film & TV Licensing

'Boogie Shoes'
Written by Harry W. Casey and Richard Finch
Performed by KC & The Sunshine Band
Courtesy of Rhino Entertainment Company
By arrangement with Warner Special Products

'Machine Gun'
Written by Milan Williams
Performed by The Commodores
Courtesy of Motown Record Company, L.P.
By arrangement with Polygram Film & TV Licensing

'Magnet & Steel'
Written by Walter Egan
Performed by Walter Egan

Courtesy of Columbia Records/Vault Vision Management
By arrangement with Sony Music Licensing and
Vault Vision Entertainment

'Craft Service Theme'
Written by J. Brion
Performed by Jon Brion, Brian Kehew,
Robin Sharp, Audrey Wiechman

'J.P. Walk'
Written by Anton Scott
Performed by Sound Experience
Courtesy of Soulville Records c/o Brookside Music Corp./
Reid Whitelaw Productions

'Got to Give It Up'
Written by Marvin Gaye
Performed by Marvin Gaye
Courtesy of Motown Record Company, L.P.
By arrangement with PolyGram Film & TV Licensing

'Ain't No Stoppin' Us Now'
Written by Gene McFadden, John Whitehead and Jerry Cohen
Performed by McFadden & Whitehead
Courtesy of Philadelphia International Records

'Driver's Seat'
Written by Paul Roberts
Performed by Sniff 'N' the Tears
Courtesy of Ace Records Ltd.

'Feel Too Good'
Written by Roy Wood
Performed by The Move
Courtesy of TRO-Muscadet Productions,
Inc. & Onward Music Ltd.

'Do Your Thing'
Written by Charles Wright
Performed by Charles Wright & The Watts 103rd St. Rhythm Band
Courtesy of Warner Bros. Records Inc.
By arrangement with Warner Special Products

'Disco Fever'
Written by Roger Webb
Courtesy of OGM Production Music

'Flying Object'
Written by Roger Webb
Courtesy of OGM Production Music

'Data World'
By Robert Ascot
Courtesy of OGM Production Music

'Queen of Hearts'
Written by Hank DeVito
Performed by Juice Newton
Courtesy of Capitol Nashville
Under license from EMI-Capitol Music Special Markets

'It's Just a Matter of Time'
Written by Clyde Otis, Brook Benton and Belford Hendricks
Performed by Brook Benton
Courtesy of Mercury Records
By arrangement with PolyGram Film & TV Licensing

'The Touch'
Written by Lenny Macaluso and Stanley Moreland Bush
Performed by Mark Wahlberg

'Feel the Heat'
Written by Paul Thomas Anderson and John C. Reilly
Performed by Mark Wahlberg and John C. Reilly

'Compared to What'
Written by Eugene McDaniels
Performed by Roberta Flack
Courtesy of Atlantic Recording Corp.
By arrangement with Warner Special Products

'O Little Town of Bethlehem'
Courtesy of Star Line Productions

'Sister Christian'
Written by Kelly Keagy
Performed by Night Ranger
Courtesy of MCA Records
Under license from Universal Music Special Markets

'Jessie's Girl'
Written by Rick Springfield
Performed by Rick Springfield
Courtesy of The RCA Records label of BMG Entertainment

'99 Red Balloons'
Written by Joem-Uwe Fahrenkrog-Peterson and Carlos Kargas
English lyrics by Kevin McAlen
Performed by Nena
Courtesy of Epic Records
By arrangement with Sony Music Licensing

'99 Luftbalons'
Written by Joem-Uwe Fahrenkrog-Peterson and Carlos Kargas
English lyrics by Kevin McAlen
Performed by Nena
Courtesy of Epic Records
By arrangement with Sony Music Licensing

'God Only Knows'
Written by Brian Wilson and Tony Asher
Performed by The Beach Boys
Courtesy of Capitol Records
Under license from EMI-Capitol Music Special Markets

'Livin' Thing'
Written by Jeff Lynne
Performed by Electric Light Orchestra
Courtesy of Jet/Epic Records
By arrangement with Sony Music Licensing

'Voices Carry' (live version)
Written by Michael Hausman, Joseph Pesce, Aimee Mann
and Robert Holmes
Performed by Til Tuesday
Courtesy of Epic Records
By arrangement with Sony Music Licensing

Soundtrack Album Available on
CAPITOL RECORDS

Special Thanks

MICHAEL ALAIMO
AMANDA ANDERSON
JOE BALL
KEVIN BRAY
KEVIN BREZNAHAN
ALEX BYRNE
BUMBLE WARD & ASSOCIATES
THELMA and KEN CARSON

MIKE DE LUCA
EDDIE DELCOUR
ALISON DICKEY
SHANA EDDY
MITCH GOLDMAN
PAUL GOUGH
MARK GRAZIANO
BOB HARVEY
PATRICK HOELCK
LOREN LAZERINE
DAVID LEE
HENRY LEE
JENNIFER JASON LEIGH
JOHN LESHER
ADAM LEVIT / ASSOCIATES IN SCIENCE
PATRICIO LIEBENSON
AIMEE MANN
ART MORGENSTERN
PALACE COSTUME COMPANY
PIE INTERNATIONAL, INC.
PAT RIDGELY
MICHELLE SATTER
RUSTY SCHWIMMER
BOB SHAYE
STEVE SHURTZ
ANDY SLATER
TIM 'STUFFY' SORONEN
MIKE STEIN
RICK STRIBLING
WENDY WEIDMAN
ALAN WERTHEIMER
JODY WOOD
MEHDI ZAMANI / RESEDA COUNTRY CLUB

Consultant
RON JEREMY

Payroll provided by
MEDIA SERVICES

Insurance provided by
NEAR NORTH INSURANCE BROKERAGE

Production Attorneys
AVY ESCHENASY
ERIK ELLNER
MARK RINDNER

Business Affairs Administrator
DAN TREINISH

Travel provided by
ALICIA THOMAS at TRAVELCORPS INTERNATIONAL

Filmed in
PANAVISION

Shot with Anamorphic Lenses.
Cut on Avid.
Filmed on Location

Dollies by
CHAPMAN

Grip and Electric by
CINELEASE, INC.

Speciality Lighting
TOWARDS 2000, INC.

Payroll Services Provided by
AXIUM PAYROLL SERVICES

Negative Cutting by
SUNRISE FILMS

Title Design
BRIAN KING

Titles and Opticals
PACIFIC TITLE

Color Timers
PHIL HETOS
JIM PASSEN

Color and Prints by
DELUXE